The Wedding Cake
Decorator's Bible

The Wedding Cake Decorator's Bible

Alan Dunn

NORTH LIGHT BOOKS
Cincinnati, Ohio
www.mycraftivity.com

A QUARTO BOOK

First published in North America in 2009 by
North Light Books. An imprint of F+W Publications, Inc
4700 East Galbraith Road
Cincinnati, OH 45236

Library of Congress Cataloging-in-Publication Data

Dunn, Alan.
  The wedding cake decorator's bible / Alan Dunn. -- 1st
American pbk. ed.
      p. cm.
  Includes bibliographical references and index.
  ISBN 978-1-60061-168-1 (pbk. : alk. paper)
1. Cake decorating. 2. Wedding cakes. I. Title.
TX771.2.D86 2009
  641.8'6539--dc22   2008042856

ISBN-13: 978-1-60061-168-1
ISBN-10: 1-60061-168-0

Conceived, designed, and produced by
Quarto Publishing plc, The Old Brewery
6 Blundell Street, London N7 9BH

QUAR.WCD

Senior editor Lindsay Kaubi
Copy editor Liz Dalby
Art editor and designer Julie Francis
Managing art editor Anna Plucinska
Art director Caroline Guest
Photographer Philip Wilkins
Illustrator Kuo Kang Chen
Picture researcher Sarah Bell
Creative director Moira Clinch
Publisher Paul Carslake

Color separation by Modern
Age Repro House Ltd, Hong Kong
Printed in Singapore by
Star Standard (Pte) Ltd

F+W PUBLICATIONS, INC.

www.fwpublications.com

Contents

Foreword

When I first started cake decorating—around 23 years ago—I owned a couple of cake decorating books, which I considered my "sugarcraft bibles," in fact, I still use them today. While I was writing *The Wedding Cake Decorator's Bible,* I had my "sugarcraft bibles" in mind, with the hope that this book becomes similarly essential to the reader.

Working on this book has been an interesting process, allowing me to feature some of my favorite techniques, as well as revisiting some that I had not used for some time; a process which has rekindled my interest in them, and prompted me to revamp them and bring them up-to-date so that they are ideal for modern wedding cake design. I have tried to include as many aspects of sugarcraft and cake decorating as I can while still focusing on those most specifically suited to wedding cake design and decoration.

The book begins with the foundations of cake decorating. Every cake needs a well-iced base; this allows the decorations to be displayed at their best, so you will find guidance on coating cakes with a range of different icings. Following this is practical advice on design considerations, a chapter of decorative methods, and a chapter dedicated to making sugar flowers. There are also useful recipes and a full set of templates for the designs used in the book.

My intention for this book is that the reader mix-and-match techniques, designs, and ideas to create their own individual wedding cake designs, sparked off by the ideas featured within these pages.

Have fun!

About this book

The book is organized into four chapters covering
the full range of wedding cake decorating options.

▶ **Foundations (pages 8–33)**
This chapter covers the basics, describing
tools and materials needed, as well as
demonstrating the core skills of coating
cakes with different types of icings.

◀ **Design (pages 34–43)**
Here, a practical approach to design is
presented with information on shape,
size, color, and flavor, as well as practical
advice on planning side designs and
using pillars.

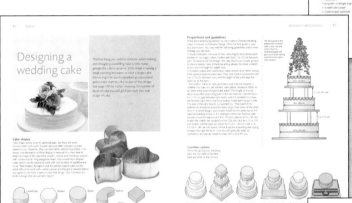

▶ **Decorative techniques
(pages 44–93)**
This chapter covers a broad range of
creative decorative techniques, from basic
piping to gelatine work, chocolate
decorations, and cocoa painting.

◀ **Sugar flowers (pages 94–125)**
Concentrating on sugar flower making, this chapter includes
core flower modeling skills as well as specific flower projects.

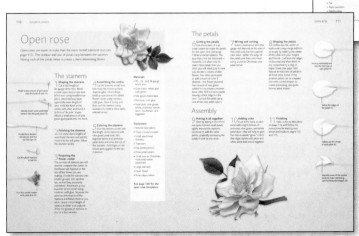

RECIPES AND TEMPLATES (PAGES 126–138)

At the end of the book you'll fine some useful recipes
as well as templates for the designs featured in the
decorative techniques chapter, and for the flowers in
the sugar flower chapter.

Covering and decorating cakes

Nonstick board and rolling pin
A dark nonstick board and rolling pin are best as these strain the eyes less than a white surface and enable you to judge the thickness of the paste.

Scissors
Scissors are useful for cutting icing bags, cutting baking parchment to line cake pans, and to cut out templates. Smaller scissors are good for cutting ribbon and small sugar items.

Spacers
Spacers are plastic rods that you can use to help give an even thickness of rolled fondant or marzipan. They can be turned two ways to result in different thicknesses.

Pastry brush
Pastry brushes can be used to spread apricot glaze over a cake surface that is to be covered with marzipan or fondant.

Icing ruler and side scrapers
A metal straight-edge icing ruler and side scraper are necessary when you are coating cakes with buttercream or royal icing. You can also buy serrated plastic scrapers that create a "combed" effect on cake sides.

Tilting turntable
A turntable that can be used upright or adjusted to a tilt is useful for coating and decorating the sides of a royal-iced or buttercream-coated cake.

Smoothers
A curved-edge smoother is wonderful for smoothing out marzipan or fondant just after it has been rolled out, and also for smoothing the top of the coated cake. A straight-edged smoother can be used on the sides of a cake to create a neat join between the cake and the board.

Dummy cakes
Polystyrene dummy cakes are available in many different shapes and sizes. They are very useful for creating the illusion of a taller wedding cake, or for occasions when a complicated design is required but the bride only wants a sponge cake. Dummy cakes are also used for display.

Palette knives
Large palette knives are useful for coating the top of a royal-iced or buttercream-coated cake—smaller ones are useful for the sides of cakes, for mixing up colored icing, and filling piping bags.

Large, flat turntable
A large, flat turntable allows easy access for decorating the top of a cake.

Cake boards

Cardboard cake boards are available from cake decorating stores and craft stores. They may be thin or drum-style and are usually coated with silver or gold paper. They should only be used once.

Metallic paper

Metallic paper is useful if you need to cover your own homemade cake boards.

Toothpicks

Good quality toothpicks are used to add paste color to icing and can also be used as a modeling or frilling tool.

Paper punches

These gadgets are wonderful for cutting out leather-hard gum paste, rice paper, or thin sheets of gelatine to add very unusual and neat touches to a design.

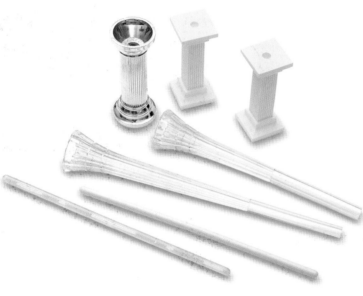

Crimpers

Shaped tweezers that press icing into interesting shapes. They are used for board edgings or as the basis for more complicated side designs.

Baking parchment, waxed paper, and acetate

Nonstick baking parchment is used for lining pans and making templates and piping bags. Waxed paper or acetate is good for piping lace and filigree designs onto.

Dowels and pillars

Dowels are used to support tiered or stacked cakes but can also be useful for a variety of decorative techniques. A variety of different styles of pillars exists for use on tiered cakes.

Pearl-head florist pins

Pins are essential for popping air bubbles on a fondant-coated cake and for securing templates. A pincushion is invaluable too to keep those pins in one place and in order!

Garrett frill cutter

These cutters are used to make frills and are available in varying sizes and with different numbers of scallops.

Embossers/patchwork cutters

There are many sugarpaste embossers available from sugarcraft stores or you can utilize leather-punches, batik imprint stamps, ink-stamps, or lace designs.

Commercial molds

There is a huge array of plastic, resin, and silicone rubber molds to choose from—some form tiny shapes that fit very well into side decoration on wedding cakes.

Lace molds

There are many commercial lace molds available made from food grade silicone rubber.

Posy/flower pick

Made from food-grade plastic—this helpful item is inserted into a cake to hold the handle of a floral spray in place.

Clay gun

A clay gun is used to extrude icing. It has various attachments, used to create different effects.

Piping tools

Store piping bags in an upright container, so they are ready on hand when needed. Once the bag is filled with icing keep the end moist and ready to work by placing it in a stand with a moist foam base. Piping tips are available in many sizes. Disposable bags can be ready-made plastic cones or made from parchment paper triangles curled into shape (see page 64).

Scriber

Use a scriber to etch designs from templates onto your iced cakes, and to mark positions for pillars.

Plastic ball tool

A modeling tool used for shaping, thinning, and curling icing.

Coloring

Coloring to add to icing is available in various types (see page 20); there are spray, gel, and paste colors, powders, liquids, and luster, as well as pens that contain edible food coloring.

Sugar flower making

Craft knife
A craft knife is essential for cutting out petals and leaves.

Plain-edged cutting wheel
A plain-edged cutting wheel is great for cutting out petal and leaf shapes and marking central veins.

Ball tool
Ball tools are available in plastic or metal—the heavier, metal ones are ideal for thinning the edges of petals.

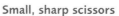

Dresden veining tool
The Dresden veining tool is a double-ended tool—one end is fine and is used to mark central veins down petals and leaves; the broad end is used to create a serrated effect to leaf edges and also for double-frilling petal edges.

Silk veining tool
A silk veining tool is a ceramic, textured tool used to texture petals and for frilling petal edges.

Fine-angled tweezers
Look for tweezers with no ridges to their grip as these will leave unattractive "teeth-marks" on your flowers. Tweezers are used to pinch ridges on petals and buds and for inserting stamens into flowers.

Cornstarch dusting bag
A cornstarch dusting bag can be made from a few layers of new diaper liners filled with cornstarch and tied together with an elastic band or ribbon.

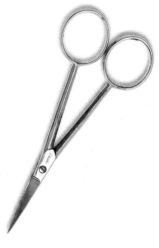

Small, sharp scissors
Small, fine, straight-edged, and curved scissors are very useful for working on fine sections of a flower. Larger scissors are good for cutting thread, stamens, and wires.

Flower and leaf cutters
There is a huge selection of cutters available from specialist cake decorating stores and on the internet or by mail order. Available in both metal and plastic, these tools help to speed up the flower-making process and create more consistent results.

Petal and leaf veiners
There is a huge selection of commercial, food-grade silicone rubber petal and leaf veiners available—these help to create natural results.

Pliers
Needle-nose pliers are used to bend hooks in wires and also help to bend and grip flowers during the assembly of flower stems and wiring sprays.

Paper-covered wires
Intended for silk and fresh flowers, paper-covered wires are used extensively in the construction of sugar flowers and foliage. White wires are most useful and are generally available from 18-gauge through to 36-gauge—the guideline is, the higher the gauge number the finer the wire. There are also brightly colored metallic wires that are useful to add color to floral and cut-out arrangements.

Petal dusts
Petal dusts are powdered food colors that will help you create stunning realistic coloring on your flowers once they are made. The powders can be dusted on dry or diluted with alcohol to create stronger coloring for patterned markings.

Edible gold and silver leaf
Sheets of food-grade gold and silver leaf can be bought in books of five, ten, or 25 from most good cake decorating stores. They are very expensive but add an instant touch of luxury and beauty to many aspects of cake design.

Paintbrushes
Fine paintbrushes for detailed work and flat synthetic fiber brushes for dusting color onto flowers and foliage.

Flower stamens
Stamens are nonedible cotton-based inserts, used for the centers of sugar flowers.

Foam pad
A foam pad can be very useful if you have hot hands. The pad enables you to work the edges of a sugar petal without the problem of the heat of your hand causing the paste to stick.

Icings

There are three basic cake icings used to cover cakes: buttercream, rolled fondant, and royal icing. Gum paste is an icing used to make intricate sugar flowers and other items.

Buttercream

Homemade or store-bought buttercream is a simple and fairly quick icing to make (see page 127 for a recipe). Butter and sugar are beaten together to form the icing—which results in a light color. There are various recipes for buttercream with a varying balance of butter to sugar. Some recipes use vegetable shortening. This results in a whiter icing but does not have the creamy taste and texture of an icing made with butter. The butter you use should be unsalted and pale in color. You can add meringue powder to create a firmer icing to pipe with (see the manufacturer's instructions for how to use it).

Uses and techniques: Buttercream can be used to fill layers of a cake and to create the coating and piped decorations. It does have the disadvantage of reacting badly in warm conditions. Many flavors can be added to buttercream with extremely satisfactory results.

Storage: Buttercream is best stored in an airtight container and refrigerated for a limited time or, better still, frozen until required. Take care not to store it near strongly flavored food, as it will pick up a taint. Allow the icing to come up to room temperature before use.

Rolled fondant

Fondant is an easy-to-use sugarpaste that is rolled out, and creates a soft, round-edged finish to a cake. Most cake decorators recommend using a ready-made, commercial fondant, as the results are more consistent and the icing easier to use. Commercial fondant is made using a boiled sugar, glucose syrup, and water mixture, with the addition of vegetable shortening, emulsifiers, stabilizers, and flavorings. Homemade recipes are mostly uncooked versions using gelatine, sugar, liquid glucose, and sometimes fresh egg whites—homemade pastes tend to dry out quickly and do not taste as good as the commercial products. Use paste or gel food colors to color white fondant.

Uses and techniques: Coating, frills, drapes, modeling (mixed with gum paste). Diluted with water, rose or orange water, or clear alcohol such as Cointreau or Kirsch, fondant can also be used for piping. Add more liquid to produce sticky sugar glue useful for attaching items to cake surfaces.

Storage: Check individual products for the "best before" date. Store at room temperature. Keep the paste wrapped in a plastic bag to prevent the surface of the paste forming a crust. Store colored fondant away from direct sunlight, as the food colors used in it are generally not lightfast.

Royal icing

Royal icing is a useful and versatile icing made by beating egg whites and icing sugar together (see page 128). Homemade royal icing is preferable to store-bought to achieve fine results. However, instant royal icing mixes to which you simply add water and beat can be useful too, especially when only small amounts of icing are required. Some cake decorating stores sell ready-made royal icing.

If your royal icing is to be used for coating a cake, you could add half a teaspoon of hygroscopic glycerine to 1 lb. (500 g) of icing. This helps to create a slightly softer icing that cuts easily. (Don't add glycerine to icing that is to be used for finer decorative purposes such as piping and lace. Add a pinch of tartaric acid instead.)

Uses and techniques: Coating, run-outs, lace, filigree, embroidery, brush embroidery, extension work, inscriptions.

Storage: Royal icing made with fresh egg white needs to be used fairly quickly, especially if it is used for lace and filigree; it often becomes weak if left for several hours. Royal icing made with dried albumen or albumen substitute can be rebeaten and used with satisfactory results. Keep it covered in an airtight container to prevent the icing crusting over.

Gum paste

Gum paste is made from confectioners' sugar, egg white, liquid glucose, gelatine, vegetable shortening, and gum tragacanth—a powder that helps to create stretch and strength. Fresh egg white, dried albumen, or albumen substitute can all be used successfully. Gum paste can be mixed in equal proportions with fondant to form a versatile modeling paste that is useful for frills and drapes. Homemade pastes can be very successful—however, more consistent results are achieved using a commercial paste.

Uses and techniques: Gum paste is excellent for making sugar flowers and can also be mixed with fondant or marzipan to create a fine modeling medium. Gum paste is also ideal for cut-out shapes, ribbons, and lace used to decorate the sides of cakes. The paste can be mixed with more fresh egg white or alcohol, water, or rose water to make a strong sugar "glue."

Storage: Gum paste can be frozen—allow it to defrost, and reknead and store it in a fresh bag to avoid sugar crystals forming a crust over the paste. Store gum paste in an airtight container and refrigerate when it is not being used. Work with the paste at room temperature.

Marzipan

Commercial marzipan is preferable to homemade marzipan, which can often be oily and crumbly to handle. A natural white marzipan is most suited to cakes that are to be coated with royal icing and fondant. (Traditionally, bakers used an artificially colored yellow marzipan because it was thought to look rich in egg yolks.) Commercial marzipan is made using blanched almonds, which are pounded, and passed through granite rollers. The almonds are then mixed with boiled sugar syrup to form a paste. Occasionally, the paste is flavored with rose or orange water, or honey. Marzipan must contain at least 25 percent almonds—otherwise it is called almond paste. (Some brands of almond paste contain over 40 percent almonds.)

Techniques and uses: Forming a firm base for royal icing or fondant. Ideal for modeling figures, flowers, and fruit; marzipan can also be used as the only coating on a cake.

Storage: Homemade marzipan can be frozen to prolong the otherwise short shelf-life. Commercial marzipans have a long "best before" date—often up to a year. Store at room temperature prior to kneading and rolling out otherwise you will find it hard to work with.

Ready-made decorations

The items pictured in this section are useful if time, energy, or skill are in short supply. They can be used to add outstanding decorative effects to wedding cakes without the commitment that many of the other sugarcraft techniques described in this book require.

Fresh flowers and herbs

Fresh flowers add instant beauty and elegance to a cake design—however, take great care to choose nontoxic blooms and foliage that has not been treated with insecticides.

Roses

In the language of flowers, white roses translate as "I am worthy of you." Whereas red roses, from the earliest times, have been associated with love. Rose petals can be used to create a very quick and pretty decoration on a chocolate- or buttercream-coated cake. This type of decoration creates a very informal display, and the petals should only be scattered at the very last minute.

Bay leaves

Bay leaves were often used to represent glory in heroes' garlands—but they can make a wonderful aromatic and bold addition to floral displays, too.

Mint

Mint is a wonderful-smelling herb that works well in fresh flower designs for cakes. Traditionally this herb symbolizes wisdom.

Moth orchids

White Phalaenopsis orchids—otherwise known as moth orchids—can make a very unusual, stunning feature in a fresh flower bouquet.

Rosemary

Rosemary symbolizes remembrance, and provides a very delicate texture suitable for use in bridal bouquets.

Violets

Violets represent modesty. They are pretty, sweet-scented flowers that work well in small bunches on a cake or as filler flowers alongside larger blooms.

Lavender

Lavender is a wonderfully calming, scented plant that is very useful for softening the edges of a spray or arrangement of flowers. It comes in several different forms and colors.

Other decorations

Silk and paper flowers

Silk or paper flowers are useful where the budget or time limit for the wedding cake is tight. Choose smaller, prettier flowers to create a more gentle design.

Dyed skeletonized leaves

Skeletonized leaves are available from most craft stores in a large range of colors. They can be combined with fresh, silk, or sugar flowers and help to give a softer feel to floral displays.

Beads

Beads and pearls make a great addition to sprays and bouquets—they can be wired and incorporated into your floral work. The example shown here can be purchased ready-wired, which makes it even easier to use.

Metallic and pearlized dragées

These edible metallic dragée decorations are available in gold, silver, pink, blue, and green. You can buy pearlized dragées from specialist cake decorating stores.

Ribbons and trims

It is wise to keep a good selection of ribbons, braids, and other trims in your design box—you never know when you will need to delve in for last-minute inspiration! Samples of fabric and ribbon can be very useful, and if you can ask the bride to supply swatches, it will make it easier for you to match colors.

Gold-coated chocolate hearts

Create a quick cake design with ready-made items such as these gold-coated chocolate hearts. You can also buy them in silver.

Feathered butterflies

Feathered butterflies can be used to add a fantasy feel to a floral display on a cake. There is a wide variety of styles available from craft stores.

Quick-fix and fun decorations

Candy

Jellybeans, lovehearts, and other candy, like marshmallows, can add fun and informal color if attached to a cake or used to fill a glass jar holding flowers.

Cake charms

Silver and gold colored plastic shoes, rings, bells, horseshoes, and so on can often be added to fill a space quickly and effectively on a cake.

Dried spices

Many dried spices have a very decorative quality to them—star anise, cardamom, and cinnamon are just a few examples that add an instant rustic charm to a winter wedding cake design.

Ricepaper roses

Ricepaper roses can add a quick fix—they are a fun, cheap, yet effective addition to a wedding cake display. They are available in assorted colors to mix and match.

Food colorings

There is a huge number of different food colorings available, making it easy for the cake decorator to achieve interesting color combinations. It is important to protect your finished creation from sunlight, or bright lights in general, to keep the colors from fading. Pinks, purples, and blues are particularly susceptible.

Liquid colors
You can use liquid colors to color royal or glacé icing. They tend to be weaker than other forms of food color and are most often used to create fairly pale, subtle colors. Most have the advantage of a droplet-type opening, which means that color can be counted drop by drop into a controlled quantity of icing. This will allow you to re-create the same depth of color in a different batch at a later stage. Liquid colors are also wonderful for painting designs onto cakes, or detailed markings onto sugar flowers and models. There are also liquid colors available that have been designed for use with an airbrush.

Paste colors
Paste colors are the most popular form of food color. They are concentrated in strength and are ideal for coloring all forms of icing. However, you need to take care not to add too much to royal icing—many of these colors are glycerol-based and this can often prevent royal-iced filigree, lace, and run-outs from drying. Paste colors may also be diluted with clear alcohol or water so that they can be used like liquid colors.

Gel colors
Gel colors are very intense, and also come in a container that allows you to measure the color drop by drop.

Nontoxic glitters
There has been a trend in recent years for adding glitter to display pieces. Although these glitters are nontoxic, they should only be used on display items that will not be consumed.

Powder colors
Dry powder food colors can be mixed into icing, but they are generally used dry, dusted onto sugar flowers and foliage to create very realistic effects. Powder colors can be diluted with alcohol and used to create more solid paint effects. They are often known as petal dusts or blossom tints.

Luster colors
Luster colors are also in powder form and can be used dry or diluted with alcohol to create a soft, subtle, shimmering finish on flowers and cake designs. Especially useful additions to your kit are bridal satin, pearl, gold, and silver. Edible luster sprays are also useful if you want to add an extra sparkle to a cake surface.

Craft dusts
Craft dusts are nontoxic but are also not edible. They are used only on items that will be removed from the cake prior to cutting, such as sugar flowers or models. The colors tend to be brighter and stronger than in food-grade dusts. Some craft dusts were originally classified as food colors, but due to changes in food regulations, the additives used in these products have to be used in controlled quantities—therefore, like nontoxic glitters, they are really only suitable for items that will not be consumed.

Food color pens
These are pens that contain food color ink. They are useful for writing messages on cakes and plaques and also for adding small details to flowers and models.

Adding color to paste

It is wise to color a smaller amount of paste (fondant, marzipan, modeling paste, or gum paste) than you need darker than required so that color can then be introduced gradually into the larger, weighed amount. This will make it easier for you to calculate how much color was used in the paste if you need to mix up another batch at a later stage.

2 Knead the color into the paste carefully—trying not to introduce large pockets of air. To create a marbled effect, simply stop kneading before the color is evenly mixed through the paste.

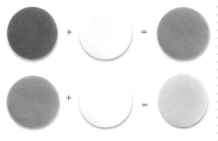

1 Dip a toothpick into the paste color and draw it across the surface of the paste—take care not to dig the stick into the paste as this may introduce pockets of air.

3 Leave the paste to rest for a few hours or overnight if time allows. This will allow you to assess the depth of color, as some tend to darken—if this is the case, simply add more white paste to the colored paste. Wrap any paste you are not using tightly in a plastic bag to keep the surface from drying out.

Mixing colors

If you want a pastel color, start with a pastel colored icing. For example, hot pink and bright yellow will not produce a soft apricot without adding a lot of white icing. In mixing soft colors, add soft colors. When trying to get exact colors, add very small amounts of color (or colored icing) until you get the color you are striving for.

Some colors that you might want to mix will require a "dulling" effect, such as moss green and dusty rose. This requires that you go to the opposite side of the color wheel. For example: leaf green plus orange equals moss green: pink plus pale green equals dusty rose.

Leaf green   Orange   Moss green

Pink   Pale green   Dusty rose

COLORING VARIABLES

There are no absolutes in mixing icing colors because of the many things that can affect the color, such as humidity, ingredients, temperature, time, and exposure to light.

Ingredients

Shortening, margarine, and butter make colors turn darker, whereas lemon juice softens colors. If you use salt in your buttercream icing, mix your colors the night before; if the salt is not thoroughly dissolved, it will leave little light spots in your icing.

Temperature and humidity

In icings that contain shortening, margarine, or butter, the temperature of the room, heat of your hands, and warmth of the liquid you add can affect the icing color. Warmth seems to make the color darken or become deeper.

Time

When using buttercream icing, soft or light colors can be made and used immediately and will only darken slightly. But when you are striving for dark colors, mix in the colors and then let the icing sit overnight before decorating: You won't have to use quite as much color. Charcoal gray will turn black, and an "almost" red will turn bright red.

Light

When your creation is finished, be careful to protect your work from sunlight or other bright lights. Pinks are especially susceptible to fading. Purples fade to blues; blues to gray; black to purple or green.

Adding color to buttercream and royal icing

Add liquid or gel colors drop by drop into a measured amount of icing. It is important to leave the icing to stand for about half an hour as the color often intensifies in these wetter forms of icing.

Coating with marzipan

Occasionally, you may be asked to make a wedding cake with a marzipan layer. A layer of marzipan helps to give a smoother finish to an iced cake and provides a very good flavor, too. It is important that the work surface is free of flour or cornstarch, as these can cause fermentation if they get trapped between the marzipan and the fondant. The marzipan coating for a fondant cake is intended to create soft curves at the edges, whereas a royal-iced cake will have square edges. It is often best—but not always essential—to leave the marzipan-coated cake for a few days to dry out and firm up prior to icing. Natural-colored marzipan is preferable to an artificial bright yellow. If you are coating the cake with several thin layers of icing, the bright yellow can often be seen through it.

Materials
- White marzipan
- Apricot glaze (see below for method)

Equipment
- Long knife
- Cake board
- Pastry brush
- Sugar shaker/sifter filled with confectioner's sugar
- Marzipan spacers (optional)
- Nonstick rolling pin large enough to roll out the marzipan to cover at least a 12 in. (30 cm) cake
- Round-edged smoother
- Straight-edged smoother
- Side scraper or flat knife
- Baking parchment

1 It is important that the cake is level—cut off the top if it has formed a dome during baking. Turn the cake upside down so that the flatter surface becomes the top. Fill any large indentations in the cake with marzipan if necessary. Place the cake onto a thin cake board the same size as the cake—this will make it easier to move. You may also add a strip of marzipan around the base of the cake to seal it and the cake board tightly together—this will depend on the individual cake edge.

2 Warm some apricot jam with a dash of water, brandy, or Cointreau and then sieve it. This makes an apricot glaze that can be painted onto the surface of the cake to help stick the marzipan to the cake and seal it to keep it fresh. Apricot glaze is used as the color is not too dark and the flavor tends not to fight with the taste of the cake or marzipan. Once you have made the glaze, use a pastry brush to apply it to the cake surface and leave it to dry.

3 It is best to store the marzipan in a warm place prior to kneading to help soften it slightly—otherwise it can be quite hard work to work with. Knead the marzipan on a clean, dry surface to make it pliable.

4 Lightly dust the work surface with confectioner's sugar. Place the marzipan on top and position spacers on either side if necessary. Rolling out marzipan to an even thickness can be tricky—plastic spacers can make this job a little easier. Depending which way they are placed, they can produce thick or thin sheets. Roll the marzipan out lengthwise using the nonstick rolling pin.

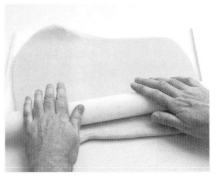

5 Turn the marzipan sideways and reposition the spacers on either side. Continue to roll out the marzipan until it is large enough to cover the cake. It is always best to allow slightly more than you think you will need, especially for difficult-shaped cakes or anything with corners.

6 Use a round-edged plastic smoother to polish and smooth out the surface of the marzipan. You will need to start off gently, gradually increasing the pressure to even out any slightly uneven areas of marzipan. Then, place the rolling pin on top of the marzipan and use it to help you lift it over the cake. Gradually remove the rolling pin and ease the marzipan into place.

7 Smooth over the surface of the cake to exclude air bubbles. Tuck in the marzipan to fit the sides. If you are working on a cake with corners, concentrate on these first of all. Make sure the sides are not pleated, and take care not to stretch the marzipan too much because it will tear and make an uneven surface. Use the round-edged plastic smoother to polish the top of the cake. Use strong, firm hand movements to even out any imperfections.

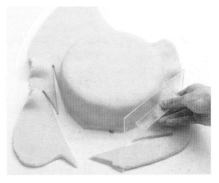

8 Use the edge of the straight-edged smoother or a flat knife to cut and flick away the excess marzipan from the base of the cake. Place the excess in a plastic bag—some of it might be reusable. Clean off the straight-edged smoother and use it to work on the sides of the cake. Try to "iron" out any creases and use the smoother to neaten the bottom edge of the cake. Place the cake on a sheet of baking parchment and leave the marzipan to firm up before coating if time allows.

Covering a cake with marzipan for royal icing

The top of the cake can be coated with a layer of marzipan and a strip of marzipan wrapped around the sides to create the square edge required for a royal-iced coating—or you can cheat slightly! Prepare the cake as described here—placing it on a thin cake board and coating with apricot glaze first.

1 Roll out a sheet of marzipan and place it on top of a board dusted with confectioner's sugar. Position the cake upside down on top of the marzipan.

2 Carefully gather the marzipan from around the sides of the cake and pull it gently up over the board that the cake is on.

3 Use a palette knife or side scraper to remove the excess marzipan. You will need to support the cake to keep the cakeboard from moving around too much.

4 Press firmly with one hand on top of the thin board and cake. Quickly work on the sides of the cake using the straight-edged smoother. You will need to press very firmly against the marzipan and cake to try and create a very square edge.

5 Place another cake board on top of the cake. Pick up the cake, holding the larger board securely. Quickly flip the cake over and remove the larger board. Smooth over the top of the cake if required. Allow the marzipan to dry for a few days before coating with royal icing.

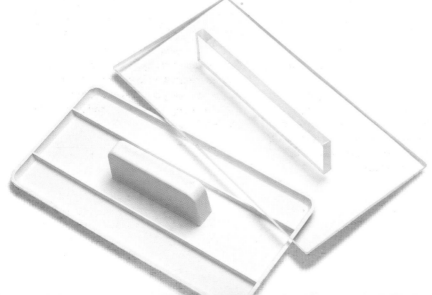

Smoothers are used to make the surface of the marzipan flat.

Coating with royal icing

Royal icing is traditionally used to cover rich fruit cakes, which have first been coated with marzipan. You will need a great deal of practice and patience to achieve a perfect coating—however, the process can be very rewarding. Ideally leave the marzipan coating (see page 22) for two or three days for the surface to harden slightly before you royal-ice the cake. If you are working in damp conditions you may have to put the cake in an airing cupboard or another warm, dry place.

Materials
• Marzipan-coated cake
• Royal icing

Equipment
• Cake board
• Turntable
• Palette knife
• Nonslip mat
• Ruler or other straight edge
• Side scraper
• Bowl
• Stainless steel smoother
• Craft knife
• Fine paintbrush

1 Place the marzipan-coated cake on a turntable. Put around two or three tablespoons of royal icing in the center of the cake with a palette knife. With a paddling motion, spread the icing toward the sides of the cake. Then, turn the cake as you tilt and rock the blade of the knife in the icing. This will even it out and eliminate any bubbles.

2 Smooth around the cake in a fan pattern, turning the cake and drawing the knife out from the center to the edges. Flatten the fan pattern in two or three sweeps, using the turntable and keeping the knife still.

3 Next, place the cake on the work surface with a nonslip mat underneath. Take a clean ruler, longer than the diameter of the cake. Hold it at either end, tilt it at an angle to the cake and pull it smoothly across the surface. Pivot the ruler so that its other long edge is in contact with the icing and swipe it firmly toward you. Maintain an even and steady pressure with both hands as you move the ruler over the cake. If after one sweep, you have not got a smooth surface, clean the ruler and repeat the process.

4 Neaten the edge of the cake top where the royal icing has fallen over the sides of the cake using a side scraper or palette knife. You will need to place the cake back on the turntable at this stage. Scrape off the excess icing and store it in a bowl for future coats.

5 To cover the sides, take some icing on the palette knife and rock it backward and forward on the cake as you rotate the turntable. Keep the knife in the icing so that it is pushed forward onto the marzipan to eliminate any air bubbles. Repeat the process until the sides are completely coated and have a reasonably smooth finish.

TIPS FOR USING ROYAL ICING

- Make up sufficient quantity of royal icing (see page 128) to give the cake three coats.
- Always keep the icing covered in an airtight container or covered with a clean, wet cloth.
- Let the top dry for about eight hours or overnight before you start to work on the sides. Do not try to dry it in an oven; the icing will discolor, and it may crack. Allow each layer of royal icing to dry for around eight hours before applying the next.
- Use "soft-peak" icing for the first coat, and then add a little water to each layer to create smoother, neater finishes.
- Work each batch of royal icing on a grease-free, nonstick board with a palette knife to remove excess air bubbles from the icing.
- Keep rulers and side scrapers clean between coatings to ensure a smooth finish.
- The cake can be coated on the board for speed; however this can affect the icing on the sides of the cake. If perfection is required it is advisable to decorate the cake and the board separately and then place them together when dry.

6 Use a stainless steel smoother to remove the excess icing from the cake sides. A plastic one might bend with the weight of the icing. Hold the smoother at an angle against the side of the cake and rotate the turntable. Smooth the sides of the cake in one continual sweep. Start with both hands on the farthest side of the cake, holding the smoother in one and the turntable in the other. Rotate the turntable toward you so that your hands meet up at their starting point. When the circle is complete, pull the smoother off gently toward you. This will leave a take-off mark, which you can etch away later using a fine craft knife.

7 Use the side scraper or palette knife to remove the excess royal icing between the sides and the top of the cake to neaten the join and maintain a square edge.

Icing the board

A better finish can be achieved by coating the cake and the board separately—however this tends to slow down the decorating process and is only really required for exhibition or competition cakes. The board would be covered in the same way as coating the top of the cake. The board needs three coats for a fine finish.

1 To cover the cake board quickly, put some icing on the board with the palette knife and turn the turntable, dragging the icing around it in short bursts until the whole surface is coated.

2 Next, use the side scraper to smooth the surface. Hold the scraper still and rotate the turntable with your other hand, smoothing all around the board in one sweep. Hold the palette knife at an angle to the board and rotate the turntable to trim off any icing the smoother has pushed over the edge. Clean off any icing from the sides of the cake board. Repeat the above steps with a slightly softer batch of royal icing for a second coat on both the top and sides, and the board. For the final, third coating, thin the icing a little more with water—this will make smoothing the icing much easier. The take-off mark from the final coating can be removed with a craft knife as before. There will be a white scratched line left on the icing—this can be removed with a slightly damp, fine paintbrush.

FROSTED, SNOWY, OR RUSTIC LOOK

If you are icing a cake for the first time and are unable to get the icing smooth, you can always turn it into rustic-style icing or create a frosted or snow-effect style. This method is also useful if you want to ice a cake in a hurry. Using unrefined golden icing sugar to make the royal icing for this style of cake can also help add to its naive charm.

- Apply the royal icing to the cake as before and use a paddling motion with the palette knife to bring it out to the edges of the cake. Pull up peaks of icing all over the cake with the side of a knife.

- Alternately, to create a lighter, more frosted look, use a slightly damp—but not wet—piece of foam sponge. This will give a lighter, more delicate texture than the knife.

- Try using a palette knife to create a swirling effect—the end result looks like the texture of a meringue nest.

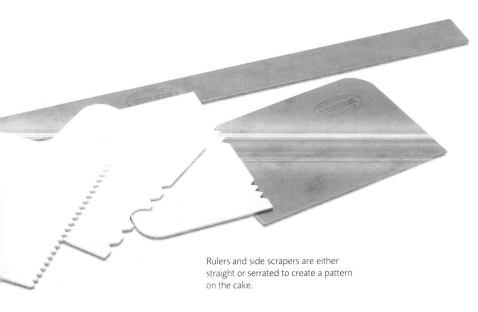

Rulers and side scrapers are either straight or serrated to create a pattern on the cake.

Coating with rolled fondant

Rolled fondant, also known as sugarpaste, is a wonderful medium for coating cakes quickly and creating a very soft, delicate base for sugarcraft designs. However, it does take quite a bit of practice to achieve a really smooth, professional finish. Fondant can be made at home; however, it is advisable and often preferable to buy a ready-made product, as the results are usually far superior and more consistent.

Materials
- Rolled fondant
- Clear alcohol (kirsch or Cointreau) or boiled, cooled water
- Buttercream or marzipan-coated cake

Equipment
- Sifter filled with confectioner's sugar
- Large, nonstick rolling pin
- Pearl-head pins
- Fondant smoothers: one round-edged and one straight-edged
- Baking parchment
- Marzipan spacers (optional)
- A makeup sponge
- Flat knife or side scraper
- Cake board

1 Knead the fondant on a clean, dry, sugar-free surface until smooth and pliable—taking care not to introduce too many air bubbles.

2 Lightly dust the work surface with confectioner's sugar and position the fondant on top, with any cracks placed against the work surface. Roll out the fondant to the appropriate size and shape needed to cover the cake. You may use marzipan spacers to help you create an even thickness (see page 22).

3 If there are any air bubbles trapped in the fondant, prick them with a pin and then use a plastic fondant smoother to disguise the hole.

4 Next, smooth and polish the surface of the fondant using a round-edged fondant smoother. This will help even out any slight rolling pin marks and create a more polished finish.

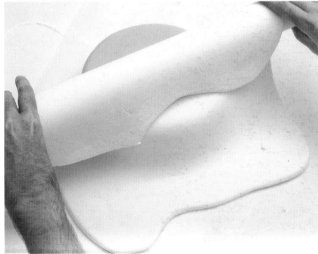

5 Place the buttercream or marzipan-coated cake onto a clean sheet of baking parchment. Quickly and evenly moisten the surface of the marzipan with clear alcohol using a makeup sponge kept just for this purpose. (A brush tends to leave dry and very wet areas causing air bubbles when the fondant is placed on top of the marzipan.) The alcohol will help the fondant stick to the marzipan and it also acts as an antibacterial agent.

6 Roll the fondant carefully onto the rolling pin and lower it over the cake, taking care to position the fondant so that it will cover the sides evenly. Remove the rolling pin and place it to one side.

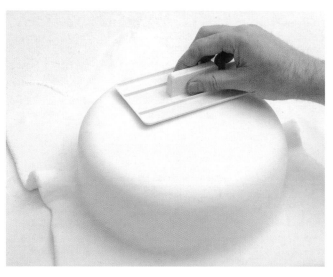

7 Next, smooth the fondant against the sides of the cake ensuring that there are no air bubbles trapped between the layers. If the cake has corners, put these in place first before tackling the sides. Avoid stretching the fondant as this will cause cracking or tearing.

8 Use a round-edged smoother to polish the top surface of the cake. Watch out for air bubbles that might be trapped between the marzipan/buttercream and the fondant—these will need to be pricked and smoothed over.

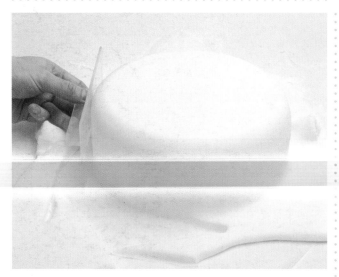

9 Smooth the sides of the cake with a straight-edged smoother (this will help you create a neat line at the base of the cake). Trim away the excess fondant from the bottom edge of the cake using a flat knife, side scraper, or even the flat edge of a fondant smoother. Flick away the excess as you work. Quickly smooth over the sides again to ensure a smooth finish and to neaten the bottom edge.

10 An extra smooth surface can be achieved with a pad of kneaded fondant placed in your palm. Use it to polish quickly all over the cake surface—particularly the edges and any difficult curves or corners that the cake might have.

TIP

It is best to use brightly colored pearl-head pins so that they can be seen easily if placed on the work surface.

COATING A CAKE BOARD WITH ROLLED FONDANT

For a neat and uniform effect, coat your cake board with rolled fondant.

1 Roll out a sheet of fondant. Moisten the cake board with clear alcohol and lift the fondant over the top.

2 Smooth over evenly using the curved plastic smoother.

3 Carefully trim away the excess fondant from the board edge using a palette knife.

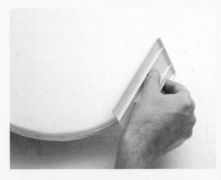

4 Smooth the edges using the smoother. Finish by polishing the surface using a pad of fondant pressed into your palm. You could add a decorative edge with a crimper, see page 50.

5 Soften a small amount of fondant with clear alcohol and smear centrally onto the coated cake board.

6 Lift the cake and position on top of the board. Press down on the top surface using a curved smoother to help secure the two together.

7 Bond and neaten the bottom edge of the cake to the board using the straight-edged smoother—care needs to be taken not to catch the surface of the cake or the board.

Coating with buttercream

Buttercream is used in a similar way to royal icing. It can be colored—it is better to use paste food colors so that the consistency of the icing is not altered. Buttercream also works well with the addition of flavorings. Although it is easier to coat the cake if the icing is at room temperature it is best to store the finished decorated cakes in cool conditions as buttercream will soften with heat.

Materials

- Sponge cake or chocolate cake
- Sugar syrup or liqueur (optional)
- Buttercream (see page 16)
- Jam or citrus curd (optional)

Equipment

- Large, flat knife
- Turntable
- Palette knife
- Icing ruler or straight edge
- Smooth side scraper
- Comb scraper (optional)
- Sharp knife

1 First, prepare the cake; it should be neat and level before you start. Trim the domed top using a large sharp knife. You can add flavored sugar syrup or liqueur to the cake for extra interest and moistness if you like (see page 130). If desired, split the cake in half or several layers and fill each layer with buttercream or a combination of buttercream and jam or citrus curd. Place the prepared cake in the freezer for about half an hour—or chill in the refrigerator for several hours. This provides a firmer base for the layers of buttercream coating.

2 Place the cake on the turntable and apply a thin first coat of buttercream to hold any loose crumbs in place. This layer is often known as the "crumb coat" and is particularly important if you are coating a dark-colored cake with a light-colored buttercream. Use a palette knife to spread a thin coat of buttercream over the top and sides of the cake. Put the coated cake back into the freezer or refrigerator again to chill before applying the next coat.

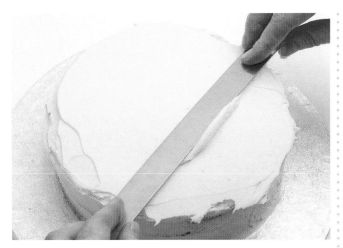

3 Remove the cake from the freezer, place it onto the turntable again, and spread another layer of buttercream over the top of the cake with the palette knife. Try not to make the layers too thick—it is easier to smooth out thin coats. Place the cake flat on the work surface. Draw an icing ruler across the surface of the icing to create a smooth surface. You might need a couple of swipes with the ruler to achieve a successful finish. Remove the excess icing from around the top edge of the cake using the palette knife. You may need a third layer of icing to create the exact finish you require—if so, refreeze the cake and coat it again.

4 Place the cake back onto the turntable. Spread another layer of buttercream onto the sides of the cake and smooth it out using the palette knife or a side scraper. To create the decorative effect shown here, use a comb scraper to texture the sides of the cake. Hold the scraper firmly in one hand and guide it carefully and smoothly around the cake, using the turntable to help you.

5 Use a sharp knife to trim the excess icing from the top edge of the cake. A piped border or crystallized flower border will hide the join around the base and the top edge of the cake. Chill the cake until it is time to serve it. Don't keep it with strongly flavored foods in the refrigerator—the buttercream will pick up the flavors, making the finished cake almost inedible.

TIPS

- When coating a square cake, work on two opposite sides of the cake, chill it, and then work on the other two sides.
- For a very smooth, bubble-free surface simply place a sheet of wax paper or food grade acetate over the surface of the cake. Smooth over the surface with your fingers and also a smoother. Freeze the cake briefly, and when you remove the cake from the freezer quickly peel off the acetate to reveal a perfectly smooth finish.

Design

Designing and decorating a wedding cake from scratch can be a daunting task, so this chapter offers guidance on the many considerations involved, including the size of the cake, color scheme, shape, whether it is to have tiers, and when to consider having a separate dummy and cutting cake.

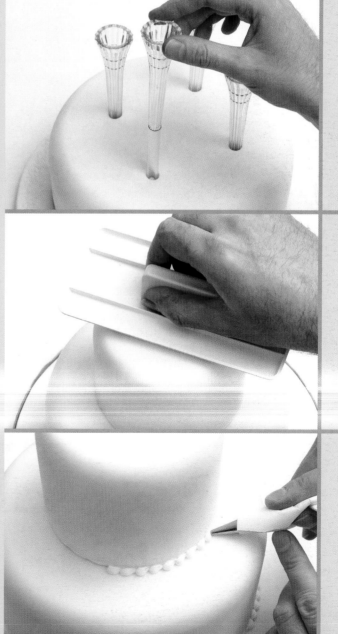

Designing a wedding cake

The first thing you need to consider when making and designing a wedding cake is how many people the cake is to serve. If the bride is having a small wedding but wants to have a larger cake, then it might be worth considering a decorated polystyrene dummy cake as part of the design. See pages 140–141 for a chart showing the number of slices of cake you will get from each size and shape of cake.

Cake shapes

Cake shape comes down to personal taste, but there are some considerations with each. Square cakes are often considered to be easiest to cut—however, they can look rather solid in tiered form. If an ornate side decoration or floral display is required, it is often best to keep the shape of the cake fairly simple—round, oval, teardrop, curved leaf, scalloped oval, long octagonal, heart, and curved heart-shaped cakes tend to be the easiest to work with and are fairly straightforward to ice. Petal shapes, hexagons, and horseshoe-shaped cakes can be more difficult to work with—some caution and thought is needed before you agree to use these shapes in your final design. Don't promise the bride a design that you will later regret!

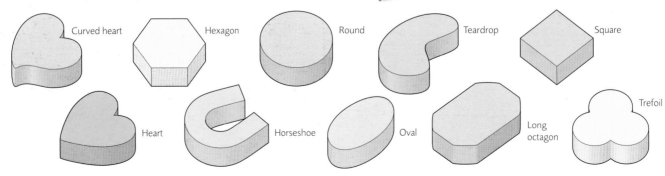

Curved heart   Hexagon   Round   Teardrop   Square

Heart   Horseshoe   Oval   Long octagon   Trefoil

Proportions and guidelines

There are traditional guidelines for the creation of tiered wedding cakes. However, as fashions change, often the best guide is your eye and instinct. You may find the following guidelines useful when making your decision:

• Royal-iced cakes, because of their often highly decorative piped borders or run sugar collars, traditionally have 2 in. (5 cm) between tiers. To balance out the design, the cake depths are usually graded to place a deeper cake at the base and gradually decrease in depth as you work through the upper tiers.

• Fondant-coated and buttercream cakes tend to look rather dumpy if the same proportions are used. They look more in proportion with 3 in. (7.5 cm) between tiers, and the depth of the cake kept the same for all the tiers.

Remember, these are only guidelines and a lot will depend on whether the cake is to be stacked, have pillars, displayed offset, or on some other type of styled cake stand. The height of the top decoration often plays a big part in this decision too. Sometimes a 4 in. (10 cm) gap between tiers works well, for example for a two-tier fondant cake where the floral display needs extra space to trail. The size of the cake boards is important too. The board of the bottom tier should be proportionately larger than those of the other tiers. In a tiered design, each board should be the same size as the cake immediately below it. For example a three-tier fondant cake would consist of a top tier of a 6 in. (15 cm) cake on a 9 in. (23 cm) board; the middle tier would be a 9 in. (23 cm) cake on a 12 in. (30 cm) board; and the base tier would be a 12 in. (30 cm) cake on a 17–18 in. (43–46 cm) board. At first it can be a daunting task trying to make the right decision—but you will gradually build up confidence and decide which formula works best for you.

The best guide to the proportions of a tiered cake is your eye and instinct but this illustrated guide will give you a solid starting point for tiered cakes with columns.

6 in. (15 cm)

2 ½ in. (6.5 cm)

8 in. (20 cm)

3 in. (7.5 cm)

10 in. (25 cm)

Countless options

When designing your wedding cake the sky really is the limit, here are some of the options.

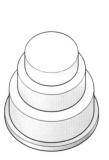

Stacked round cakes

Tiered square cakes with columns

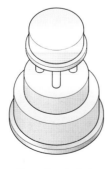

Two cakes stacked with a final top tier on pillars

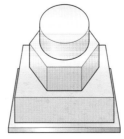

A square, hexagon, and round cake stacked

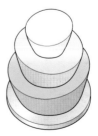

Topsy-turvy stacked tiers

Novelty suitcase and hat box cake

Cutting the cake

If a design requires the inclusion of polystyrene dummy cakes, then you might suggest that you create a "display" cake using the iced dummy cakes, and separate "cutting" cakes to keep in the kitchen that can be served to the guests. This also takes away the worry of creating a cake containing several different flavors or types of cakes, or is helpful if you need to complete the cake design well in advance of the wedding. You could also suggest that fruit cakes are sliced in advance, wrapped in wax paper and then decorative tissue paper, and tied with bows. These pre-wrapped slices can also look good presented to one side of the main decorated display cake and scattered with rose petals. This will allow the guest to take the cake home to eat at a later stage—an idea that might be welcomed after a large meal.

Dummy cakes

Avoiding waste

There is much less waste if a cake is cut in slices as illustrated below, rather than in wedges.

Pre-wrapped
cake slices

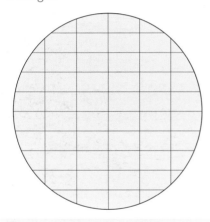

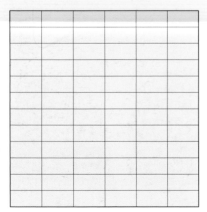

WHAT FLAVOR?

Wedding cakes need to be sturdy enough to take heavy layers of icing, and decorations, so a high-density sponge or fruitcake is ideal (see pages 130–131 for cake recipes). Carrot cake and chocolate cake are also popular choices and you could even have a three-tier cake with a fruit layer, a sponge layer, and a chocolate layer. Sponge cakes can also be flavored with many different things. Alternatively, why not opt for a display of individually decorated cupcakes?

Side designs

When you are designing a tiered cake, keep in mind the depths of the cakes if you are using piped embroidery or lace. When decreasing the depth of each tier, it is important to decrease the lace and embroidery designs proportionately too, or it will result in a heavy overall display. Samples of embroidery or lace can be copied from the bride's dress or simplified and included in these side designs.

Color schemes

This is often something that is taken out of your hands. The bride's or bridesmaids' dresses and flowers are often chosen long before the cake is even considered. It is often best to try and get as much information as possible from the bride regarding types and colors of flowers. Swatches of fabric and ribbons can be useful too.

POPULAR COLOR SCHEMES

White
Baby blue
Pale green
Lavender
Peach
Baby pink
Cream
Baby yellow

Sugar flowers

These are most often used as the starting point for a cake design. The bride or florist might contribute to fairly complicated color schemes and floral combinations. It is often best to choose only a selection of the bride's flowers to be included in the design, and you might need to introduce other, simpler, sugar flowers to make a design work on a cake. Try to be realistic about what you can create with your level of skill, the time you have available, and—most importantly—the budget you are working to. See pages 96–125 for guidance on making sugar flowers.

Fresh flowers

If fresh flowers are requested, it is important that you obtain flowers that have been grown without harmful insecticides and that the varieties you are using are not toxic. If fresh flowers are requested that are toxic, you should suggest the use of dummy cakes and provide separate cutting cakes.

TIP

Make a rough sketch on paper, or even imagine in your mind how you envision the cake will look—but don't be afraid to take another direction if your original plans don't work or if you start to follow an unplanned instinct—this is all part of the creative process. Making a simple sketch of your idea can be really helpful as illustrated below.

Templates

Sometimes a side design will require that you make a template either to mark the design onto the surface of the cake coating, or to divide it into curved sections ready to apply piped lace or a frill. If you plan to use the same designs again in the future, keep them together in a folder. Designs can take inspiration from greeting cards, invitations, the bride's dress fabric, or embroidery pattern books.

Materials
- Coated cake

Equipment
- Turntable
- Measuring tape
- Sharp scissors
- Baking parchment
- Pencil
- Curved ruler
- Pin or masking tape
- Scriber

Scalloped side template

1 Place the coated cake onto a turntable. Measure the circumference of the iced cake with the measuring tape. Cut a strip of baking parchment the same length as the circumference.

2 Divide the measurement by the number of sections you need for the design. Mark the paper using a pencil at the required intervals. Fold the strip of baking parchment into the measured sections. Mark the depth required onto both edges of the paper and use a curved ruler to draw in the scalloped pencil line.

3 Cut out the scalloped shape. Unfold the strip of baking parchment and wrap it around the cake. Hold in place with a pin or a piece of masking tape.

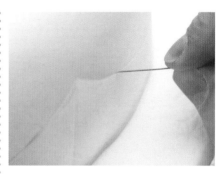

4 Use a pin or a scriber to etch the scalloped design into the surface of the cake coating. Try not to be too heavy-handed as this line might show when you attach delicate pieces of lace to the design.

Sharp scissors are useful for cutting out templates and a scriber for etching designs onto icing.

5 The finished design adds a simple yet elegant look to the cake.

Positioning pillars

The exact position of the pillars will depend on the size of the top tier, the board it is sitting on, and also the display of flowers or decoration that is planned. The instructions below can be used as a guideline for positioning pillars—but a lot will depend upon the design of the cake.

Materials

- Coated cake
- Pillars

Equipment

- Measuring tape
- Sharp scissors
- Baking parchment
- Pencil
- Scriber
- Spirit level

1 Take a tracing of the surface of the coated cake using a sheet of baking parchment, fold the template into quarters, and mark the distance of the pillars from the center of the cake.

2 Unfold the template and position it on top of the cake. Scribe the position of each pillar onto the icing.

3 The pillars shown here are tapered and can be inserted directly into the cake. Push them in so that they go through the depth of the cake and touch the cake board. You could check that they are level using a small spirit level.

4 Position the smaller tier to sit centrally on top of the pillars.

CALCULATING PILLAR POSITIONS

This diagram shows you how to work out where to position pillars on a round cake but the principles involved for most cake shapes are the same. Templates can be made from paper or card. To obtain a good shape in either case, either draw around the cake tin and cut out the shape just inside the line to allow for the thickness of the tin, or make a paper pattern following the instructions (see right). You can use either three or four pillars, it's just a matter or deciding which looks best.

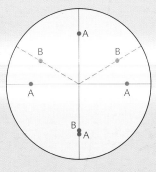

A round cake can either have four pillars on the cross (A) or three pillars on the triangle (B). For the cross, fold into four, open and mark points (A) on the folds. For the triangle, fold in half and mark the first position (B) the correct distance from the center of the cake according to the chart (see left). Fold into three making an angle of 60°, and mark the second position (B) on the outside fold; open up and mark the third point (B) on the third fold. These same principles can be applied to most cake shapes.

Size of cake	Distance of pillar from center
8 in. (20 cm)	2½ in. (6.5 cm)
10 in. (25 cm)	3 in. (7.5 cm)
12 in. (30 cm)	3½ in. (9 cm)
14 in. (35 cm)	4 in. (10 cm)

Doweling a cake

Some styles of pillars and separators will require the cakes to be doweled to support the weight of the cake above. The dowels are cut to the height of the pillars and the cake combined. The pillars are then placed over the dowel to conceal them. Stacked cakes also require dowels, but the dowel need only be cut to the exact height of the cake. Dowels can be purchased from cake decorating stores—they are made from white or clear plastic, or wood.

Materials
- Coated cake tiers (two different sizes)
- Royal icing or softened fondant
- Ribbon (optional)

Equipment
- Dowel
- Sharp pencil
- Sharp scissors or hacksaw
- Plastic smoothers
- Piping bag and tip (optional)

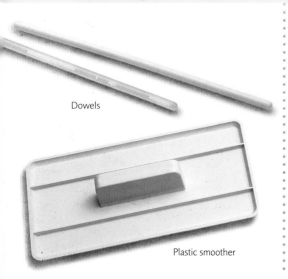

Dowels

Plastic smoother

1 Insert the dowel into the cake and make a mark slightly above the level of the cake's surface with the pencil. For a tiered cake, add the height of the pillar to this measurement, and record.

2 Remove the dowel and cut to the required length using sharp scissors or a hacksaw. Repeat this process for the other dowels needed.

3 Use a plastic smoother to apply weight to make sure the dowels are pushed into the cake evenly.

4 Pipe or dab some royal icing or softened fondant on top of the cake and carefully place the smaller tier on top.

5 Use smoothers to press onto the top tier to secure it in place. If the fondant is still soft on the top tier you will be able to use a straight-edged smoother to neaten and blend the join between the two cakes.

6 Attach a band of ribbon around the join or pipe a snail trail or shell border to disguise the join.

Securing flowers to a cake

Securing a spray of flowers to the top of a cake is a simple process: use a posy pick, bought from cake decorating suppliers.

Materials
- Posy pick(s)
- Clear alcohol
- Flower spray(s): fresh or gum paste

Equipment
- Long tweezers or needle-nose pliers

1 You can buy posy picks from speciality cake decorating stores—they are made from food-grade plastic. Sterilize the pick by wiping it with clear alcohol. Decide where the spray of flowers is to be positioned and carefully insert the pick into the cake. It is best to have the top section of the pick showing so that it can be retrieved easily prior to the cake being cut.

2 Insert the handle of a wired spray of fresh or sugar flowers into the posy pick. (For very large bouquets of flowers where the handle of the spray will not fit in a posy pick, cut a tapered plastic crystal-effect pillar down to the required depth and use it in just the same way as a pick.)

DISPLAYING WEDDING CAKES

Candleholders can make an interesting alternative to the more traditional wedding cake display and help you create a more individual look. Make sure the holder is strong enough to hold the weight. Position the smaller, top tier on top of the candleholder and elevate the base tier slightly by placing a smaller cake board underneath the baseboard. This type of positioning will allow more room for floral displays or modeled figures and will also take away the worry of having to insert dowels into the cake.

Tilted cakes

Flexi-glass or plastic tilted cake stands can help to create a more interesting design. However, it is best to use only display polystyrene dummy cakes for this purpose! A real cake can be tricky when tilted. The stand comes with plastic pins that are pushed through the stand into the underside of the dummy cake.

3 Once the spray is positioned in the posy pick you will need to "relax" the flowers and foliage into place using long tweezers or needle-nose pliers.

Decorative techniques

This chapter is the largest in the book and covers a wide variety of techniques—both traditional and with a more up-to-date twist—that will help to inspire and spark off the creative process for both the novice and more experienced cake decorator.

Modeled rose

This style of rose is ideal for the novice cake decorator, or if you need to fill a large surface area quickly on a wedding cake. As there are no wires, these flowers are great to use on cakes that are intended to be eaten. This method works equally well with fondant, chocolate paste, gum paste, modeling paste, or—as shown here—with marzipan. The only problem with this method is that if you have hot hands the roses tend to become very sticky—therefore, it is recommended that you mold the petals between two layers of plastic.

Materials
- Marzipan
- Food coloring: pink, leaf green

Equipment
- Dark colored nonstick board
- Toothpick
- Plastic bag
- Sharp knife
- Dresden veining tool
- Fresh rose leaf or silicone-rubber rose-leaf veiner

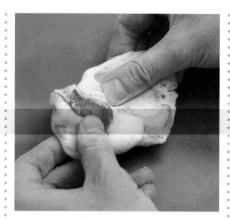

1 If using marzipan, knead to soften it slightly and make it more pliable. Use a toothpick to add food coloring to the marzipan. Carefully knead the marzipan, making sure the color is evenly mixed through. Wrap the marzipan in a plastic bag and leave it for a couple of hours to rest. The color tends to become darker on resting—so this will allow you to assess it before you make the flower.

2 Break off a piece of your chosen modeling paste, knead it slightly, and then roll it into a ball between your palms. You will find that having a clean, damp cloth at hand is very useful throughout the modeling process.

3 Apply pressure to one side of the ball, working the paste between your palms to form an elongated teardrop, or cone shape. Squeeze the cone toward the base to form a "waistline" and create the basic platform to add the rose petals onto (see completed platform in Step 6).

4 Next, start to form the petals—roll four equal-sized balls of colored paste.

5 Place one of the balls into a plastic bag. Close the bag and press the ball down to flatten it and start to form a rounded rose-petal shape. Thin the edges of one side of the petal by applying pressure with your finger.

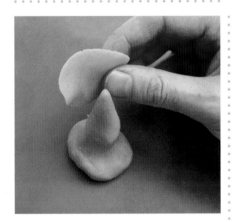

6 Position the petal on the cone so that it is higher than the tip. Tuck in the left-hand side of the petal tightly so that it hides the tip of the cone.

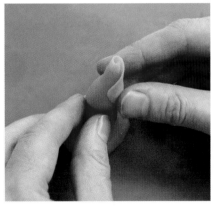

7 Continue to spiral the petal around to form a tight, neat center. The marzipan will stick to itself easily—you will need to use water or alcohol to stick the petals of a fondant rose together. At this stage you might decide to create a bud, in which case curl the edge of the petal back slightly.

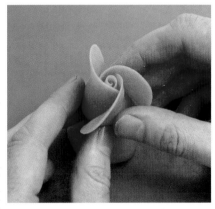

8 Repeat the process with the other three petals. Position the first petal over a join, sticking down one side tightly against the cone. Attach the remaining two petals to form a spiral shape. Keep the petals open at first so that you can position them correctly.

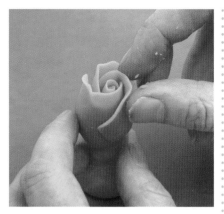

9 Gradually tighten each of the petals and curl back the edges for a more realistic finish. Pinch an angle at the center of each petal to create a little more interest in the shape of the rose. You could stop at this stage if you decide to create an open bud shape. If you decide to continue, you may want to lighten the color—if so, mix equal amounts of white paste together with the colored one.

10 Roll three balls of the lighter paste— slightly larger than before—and repeat the thinning out process as for the previous rose petals.

11 Add the three petals as for the previous layer, but this time try to open up the shape a little more, to allow the petals to "breathe." Curl back the edges using your fingers.

12 Once again, add an equal amount of white paste to the lightened colored marzipan. Roll five slightly larger balls of marzipan and repeat the thinning process as before. Start attaching the petals around the rose, positioning the first one of this layer over a join. Place the next petal on the opposite side of the flower, again over a join, and so on.

13 Continue to add the remaining three petals, curling back their edges as you attach them. Pinch a vein at the center of each petal to create a more realistic effect. Squeeze or cut the rose off the platform at the base. If the rose is very large you might need to support the petals with tissue paper or absorbent cotton.

Making the leaves

1 The leaves can also be molded in a similar way, but using a cone-shape of leaf-green colored marzipan. Thin out the shape at the edges, forcing the cone to take on a leaf shape. The paste at the center needs to be a little thicker to support the leaf.

2 Add a serrated edge, using the fine end of the Dresden veining tool to "bite" into the edge of the leaf.

3 Texture the leaf for a realistic effect, using either a fresh rose leaf or a double-sided silicone-rubber leaf veiner.

4 Pinch the leaf at the tip to create movement and position it behind the finished rose. Leave to dry.

Crimper work

Crimpers—sometimes called nippers—are available in a wide variety of shapes and widths. Some crimpers have serrated edges, giving almost a "teethmark" edge to each shape. Crimper work must be done on a freshly coated fondant or marzipan cake. The shapes can be used on their own to create border designs or combined to make feature designs. Crimper work can also be effectively combined with embroidery, painted designs, lace, ribbon work, and embossing, and can be overpiped with royal icing. Crimpers are also useful for disguising the join between a Garrett frill and a cake. Practice the crimper design on a scrap piece of icing prior to completing the design on the cake.

Materials
- Fondant or marzipan-coated cake
- Silver or gold leaf (optional)
- Luster gels (optional)
- Petal dust food colors
- Cocoa butter (optional)
- Clear alcohol
- Gum paste
- Metallic or pearlized dragees
- Silver or gold leaf (optional)
- Royal icing

Equipment
- Assorted crimpers
- Paintbrushes
- Piping tips (optional)

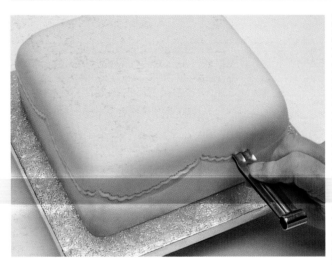

Crimped detail
Crimpers are wonderful for adding a little extra detail to the edge of a fondant-coated board. Place the board onto a turntable so that you can quickly turn the board around, holding the crimpers in one place to complete the design.

Creating a scalloped design
To create a scalloped crimper design around a cake you will first need to make a template to wrap around the cake (see page 40). Use an elastic band if you need to control the aperture of the crimper—the wider the aperture the more ridged the final crimper marks will be. Adjust the aperture by sliding the elastic band higher or lower along the crimper. To create the design, insert the crimpers into the fondant, pinch them together, release, and move them away from the design. If you forget to release the crimpers, a section of the fondant will be damaged. You might need to dust the crimpers with cornstarch if the fondant is too sticky.

Simple design

This design was created using a double-scalloped crimper. Sometimes a cake needs only a small amount of added design—this is where crimpers are useful for adding decoration to boards or the sides of a cake.

Hearts

A heart crimper works well when creating a repeat design. The hearts have been painted using colored cocoa painting techniques (see page 82) and dots of piped luster gel.

Frame

Two bands of ribbon work well to frame a simple oval crimper-work design. Further interest is added with tiny flowers and leaves painted with a mixture of petal dusts and clear alcohol.

Abstract design

A crimped line has been repeated to create the base of this design. The lines were then painted with luster dusts mixed with clear alcohol and then tiny dots of blue luster gel and silver leaf/gum paste flakes added.

Lively side design

A scalloped oval crimper forms the base of this brightly painted side design. Silver dragées are used at the center of each section and then clear alcohol and brightly colored petal dusts are used to complete this lively design.

Blue pearls

A wavy crimper is the base of this design. Blue pearlized dragées are attached at intervals with small dots of royal icing and the crimper work is highlighted with blue luster dust mixed with clear alcohol.

Zigzag

Using a v-shaped crimper in repetition forms a quick zigzag design. A small piping tip is used to emboss (see page 54) tiny dots. The design can be left uncolored but in this instance the zigzag and the dots have been highlighted with food color.

Frills and flounces

The basic frill is known as the Garrett frill, after its South African inventor. It entails pressing a toothpick at close intervals into a scalloped frill to produce an almost "smoked" type of finish. It was later discovered that you could actually just as easily roll the toothpick to make prettier, lighter frills, or flounces. Frills and flounces can be made using only fondant—however, it is possible to create a finer effect if you add up to 50 percent gum paste to the fondant. This also tends to make the frill set quickly in the correct position. Frills may be used in single or multiple layers to create a simple, or a more fluffy, effect.

Materials
- Fondant and gum paste: 50/50 mix
- Cornstarch dusting bag
- Royal icing
- Fine ribbon

Equipment
- Nonstick board and rolling pin
- Garrett frill cutter
- Toothpick
- Small sharp craft knife
- Paintbrush handle
- Piping bag and very fine piping tip

Garrett frill cutters are available in varying sizes and with different numbers of scallops. Some have different-sized circle cutters so that you can alter the depth of frill—the larger circle cutters produce shallower frills.

Making a Garrett frill

1 Roll out the fondant/gum paste very finely on a light dusting of cornstarch. Cut out a frill shape using your chosen size of frill cutter. Open up the circular frill and carefully straighten it out a little.

2 Lightly dust the board with more cornstarch. Take a toothpick and start to press indents into each scalloped section. Here, the toothpick has been angled to create a triangular, pointed shape. As you work, flick up each frill.

Making a flounce

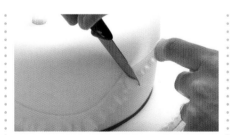

1 To create a flounce, proceed as for the Garrett frill, but this time roll each section firmly using the toothpick—a light dusting of cornstarch on the frill helps to keep the toothpick from sticking.

2 Moisten the scribed line on the side of the cake with water. Turn over the left-hand edge to create a neat start to the frill, then attach to the moistened line. Use a craft knife to trim the flounce to fit the design.

3 Next, use a paintbrush handle to lift each section of the flounce to create a more airy feel. To neaten the top edge of the flounce, pipe tiny royal icing dots onto it. Add ribbon bows at the join of each scallop, using small dots of royal icing to fix them.

Disguise the join!
A single scalloped frill can be crimped along the top edge using a scalloped crimper to disguise the join between the cake and the frill. See crimper work, page 50.

Detailed design
Adding a simple combination of piped embroidery, eyelet holes, and a fine snail trail along the top edge of a flounce can help to create a more detailed and gentle design for the sides of a cake.

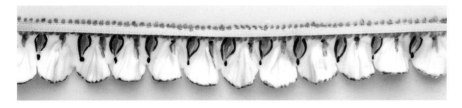

Colorful effects
Here, a simple straight frill has been decorated with a band of ribbon. Catch the edge of the frill with a diluted mixture of green petal dust luster and clear alcohol. You will need a steady hand for this job!

Rosebuds
A delicate, painted rosebud design is added once the frill has had some time to dry. A fine paintbrush, petal dust diluted with clear alcohol, and a careful eye and steady hand are needed to paint all of the frills around a whole cake.

Double frill
Two layers of scalloped frill are used here. The underfrill is made using pink paste and the top frill is white to match the main coating. Crimp, pipe dots, attach blossoms or hearts, or simply paint an alternate dotted design as pictured here.

Embossing

Embossing is an effective technique that is ideal for novice cake decorators. It can be used to create decorative side designs on a cake or around the edge of a coated cake board. It is also wonderful for covering up a poor fondant coating or for creating a simple design onto a marzipan-coated cake. Create designs using something as simple as a plastic doily or piping tips, or achieve more interesting results using leather punches, buttons, or plastic embossers from speciality cake decorating stores. Work directly onto a cake, or make fondant plaques that can be embossed well in advance and used to create effective designs on those inevitable last-minute cakes!

Materials
- White fondant
- Petal dust: white, pink, turquoise, and purple
- Clear alcohol

Equipment
- Butterfly embossers/cutters
- Piping tips (various sizes)
- Dusting brushes
- Fine paintbrush
- Decorative button, leather punch, or embosser
- Lace, batik stamp, or petal cutters (optional)

1 While the fondant is still soft, quickly press the butterfly embosser into it. Be firm and confident in your application—do not jiggle the embosser or try to emboss twice, as this will be difficult to color later.

2 Quickly work through the varying sizes of butterfly embossers to create a varied and interesting fantasy design.

3 Use plain piping tips in varying sizes to create a freestyle "bubble" effect to soften the edges of the design.

4 Use a flat dusting brush and a mixture of white and pink petal dusts to "blush" each butterfly, from the central body through the wings. Decrease the amount of color as the butterflies decrease in size.

5 Use turquoise and white petal dusts to color the bubbles and the tips of the wings. Dilute some purple dust with clear alcohol and, with a fine paintbrush, color in the main bodies, adding an outline and finer detail following the embossed pattern.

6 Use a decorative button, leather punch, or an embosser to create a pretty decorative edge to a coated cake board.

Silk effect

This texture is achieved using a silk textured rolling pin developed for the sugarcraft market. Extra effect is added using a dusting of pearl luster food color. Drag the bristles of the brush over the ridges of the design.

Dragonflies

This pretty design is made using a rubber stamp to emboss the sugarpaste coating. Allow the sugar to dry before painting gently with blue and green luster food colors mixed with clear alcohol.

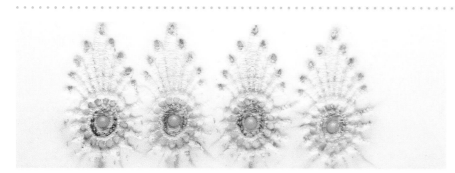

Lace feathers

This repeat design was made using a single section of a piece of lace—held upside down and pressed into the paste to create a delicate design. Pearl dragées are attached at the center of each section. The remainder is then dusted with gold and green luster food colors. Stronger detail is painted using clear alcohol and the green luster dust to create a peacock feather effect.

Paisley

A batik stamp is used here to create a very bold and instantly eye-catching design. A little time and patience is needed to add painted details to each section of the design.

Daisy chain

This simple embossed design is made using a tiny daisy petal cutter, available from most good cake decorating stores. Fine painted detail is added using a very fine paintbrush. Connect each daisy head together with a simple leaf and dot design.

Flower scroll

This design is embossed using a sugarcraft embosser. Each section is painted using clear alcohol and petal dusts. The purple outline is done with a purple food color pen. Add dots in purple and red to link.

Cut-outs

There are many kinds of cutters—available from cake decorating stores—designed specifically to create quick and effective cut-out side designs. You can also use flower and leaf cutters to make designs that complement the floral displays used on the tops of wedding cakes. More recently, cake decorators have started to use paper punches to cut out sugar designs—giving an even larger array of different shapes to work with. Edible gold and silver leaf can also be used to coat the paste prior to cutting out the various shapes, adding a touch of glamour and luxury to any cake design.

Materials
- Vegetable shortening
- Chosen color of gum paste
- Gold or silver leaf
- Cornstarch dusting bag
- Assorted petal dusts (optional)

Equipment
- Nonstick board and rolling pin
- Paper towel
- Cranked palette knife
- Dusting brush (optional)
- Paper punch
- Fine paintbrush

See page 132 for the cut-out templates.

Making gold and silver leaf cut-outs

1 Roll out some well-kneaded gum paste very thinly onto a greased nonstick board using a small nonstick rolling pin. Use a cranked palette knife to carefully release and lift the paste from the board.

2 Open up a book of gold or silver leaf and carefully lower the sticky side of the paste onto a sheet of the metal. Use your fingers or a large clean, dry dusting brush to apply pressure to the paste to help bond the two materials together.

3 Peel back the paste from the paper in the book to reveal the metal leaf-coated paste. If you are intending to use a paper punch, leave the paste to set for an hour first; but if you are planning to use a flower cutter cut the shapes out straight away.

4 Place the firm sheet of coated paste into the slot of the paper punch. Press firmly on the lever to punch out the shape. Repeat to cut out the required number of shapes.

Finished design
Try combining several assorted shapes to create an individual design. The dragonfly and fishhook shapes in this design were also cut out with paper punches. The white paste was dusted with purple petal dust prior to the shapes being cut out.

Silver dragonflies

These charming silver-leaf/gum paste dragonflies have been cut out using a tiny paper punch. A plain medium piping tip is used to cut out the silver flower centers. Extra dotted detail has been added using a fine paintbrush, clear alcohol, and petal dust food colors.

Silver hearts

Grains of lavender sugar crystals have been rolled into the surface of a sheet of silver leaf/gum paste to add extra color, texture, and detail. A curved heart cutter was used to cut out the main element of the design. A cocoa painted rose and dots help to create a more interesting side design.

Folk art

This unusual shape is cut out using pale pink gum paste. Colored cocoa butter is then painted in layers onto the cut-out shapes and extra dots and leaf designs help to create a more individual motif.

Gold and purple hearts

These cut-out hearts were all made with purple colored gum paste with lavender sugar crystals rolled into the paste to add texture. Two of the hearts also have a layer of gold leaf sandwiched between the paste and the crystals.

TIP

There will be leftover bits of paste once the main designs have been cut out—to utilize the metal leaf-coated paste, try cutting out small "dots" of paste using plain-edged piping tips of various sizes. Or, try leaving the paste to dry thoroughly and then break up the leftover paste into bits. These small "dots" or "eggshell" bits can be used as side decorations on their own (see "Abstract design," page 51), or threaded onto a wire to add to wired sugar flower sprays.

Simple blossoms

This simple design was cut out using the blossom template on page 136. In this design they are used flat against the cake but they could be shaped. A purple food color pen was used to add dotted flower centers and extra detail to the edges of the design.

Stenciling

Stencils can be used to create a fairly quick decoration on a cake or even on the cake board itself. There is a vast array of stencils available for sugarcraft purposes and even more for home decorating. Stencils can be used directly on a coated cake or on fine sheets of gum paste, which can then be cut around and attached to the cake. The stenciled design can be created with dry petal dusts, or with alcohol-diluted colors and a stencil brush, or even with color mixed with vegetable shortening for a more controlled application.

Materials
- White gum paste and fondant mix
- Assorted petal dusts
- Clear alcohol/cooled boiled water

Equipment
- Nonstick board and rolling pin
- Stencil
- Dusting brushes
- Photographer's puffer or empty, clean shampoo bottle
- Craft knife

See page 132 for the stenciling templates.

1 Mix equal amounts of white gum paste and fondant. (This will give the fondant a little more stretch and strength.) Roll out the paste on a nonstick board to the required thickness—it is best to roll the paste quite fine, but this will depend on the size of your design.

2 Turn the paste over so that the "sticky" side that was against the board is now uppermost—this will help the stencil to grip while you use it. Place the stencil on top of the paste and smooth it in place with your fingers. This is a commercial stencil; you should be able to get something very similar in a cake or home decorating store.

3 Use a soft, firm dusting brush to apply color to the stencil design. Be careful not to use too much color as this will have to be removed before the stencil is lifted. The temptation is always to blow the dust off the paste—but choose the hygienic option of using a photographer's "puffer" or an empty, clean shampoo bottle to blow the dust away instead.

4 Continue to add more colors to the design. Once you have achieved the desired effect, carefully peel back the stencil and set it aside.

5 Use a craft knife to cut around the design. Use the entire stenciled shape or cut it into sections to suit the finished cake design.

6 Moisten the back of the stenciled design with a little clear alcohol or cooled, boiled water and position it on the cake.

Petal dusted design

This double poppy design has been created using the techniques described opposite. The colors are applied in layers, mixing a little white into pink petal dust to create a strong base color and then gradually adding more depth with full strength dust.

Burgundy rose

A simple rose stencil has been used to create a repeat design suitable for the side of a cake. The petal dusts have been mixed with white vegetable shortening—although melted cocoa butter could also be used to create a thick "paint" (see page 82). When applied to the stencil, the vegetable fat creates a more textured final effect.

Paisley design

A commercial paisley stencil was used here to create a bold feature design. Once the petal dust colors have been added to the design try highlighting the areas with a diluted mixture of clear alcohol and gold petal dust to create a more interesting result.

Royal-iced paisley

Pale pink royal icing has been spread over a large stencil design to create a textured flock wallpaper effect. Once the icing has set, simply brush over the raised areas of the design with a luster dust, which helps to soften the design.

Curlicues

A curled stencil is used to create a simple base to this unusual design. Adding painted effects to the design gives more depth and dimension.

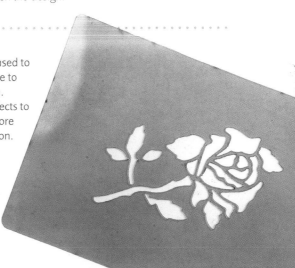

Gelatine work

Gelatine can be used to create interesting decorative touches in cake design. Flowers made from gelatine are fairly strong but also very lightweight. You need a little patience if you are planning to use gelatine cut-outs; it can take a few days for a thin sheet of gelatine to set firmly enough to be cut.

Materials

- Four sheets of leaf gelatine
- Three tablespoons of cold water
- Paste or liquid food color (optional)
- Acetate
- Gold or silver leaf (optional)
- Melted gelatine mixture
- Fine paper-covered or colored wire
- Nile green florist tape
- Gum paste
- 26-gauge wire
- Prepared gelatine wings
- Clear alcohol
- Petal dusts or bridal satin dusts
- Nontoxic glitter
- Nontoxic glue

Equipment

- Small bowl
- Tablespoon
- Craft knife
- Pan
- Paper punches
- Paintbrushes

These are the materials and equipment needed for all of the gelatine techniques.

Gelatine cut-outs

1 Break up four sheets of leaf gelatine and place them in a small bowl. Add three tablespoons of cold water. For colored effects add paste or liquid food color to produce clear, shiny gelatine work. Or, for a more papery feel, add petal dusts and bridal satin dusts. Stir in the color and leave it to dissolve for 30 minutes. Next, place the gelatine mixture over a pan of just-boiled water to melt it slightly and make it thinner and easier to use. Try not to stir the mixture too much as this will encourage air bubbles, that will show in the final work.

2 Spoon some of the melted mixture onto a sheet of acetate. Pour off the excess and set the mixture aside for two or three days. When it is set completely, you should be able to peel off the thin sheet of gelatine.

3 Use paper punches to cut out shapes that can be used on the sides of a cake design. Try pouring gelatine onto gold or silver leaf and leaving it to set to create another interesting finish.

Gelatine flowers

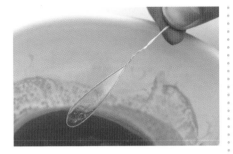

1 Make petal- and leaf-like frames with the wire. Dip the frames into the melted gelatine mixture to create a very fine, bubble-like coating. It might take a few tries to achieve a successful finish. If there are air bubbles in the melted gelatine, these will be visible on the finished pieces.

2 Allow the gelatine petals to dry for a few hours before taping them together to form abstract flower shapes.

Dragonfly

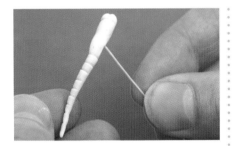

1 Form the body of the dragonfly using gum paste. Create a series of lines on the lower half of the body and divide the head section to form two eyes. Insert a hooked, moistened 26-gauge wire into the upper half of the body. Leave it to dry.

2 Tape four gelatine wings onto the sides of the dragonfly body using quarter-width florist tape.

3 Mix together some clear alcohol and iridescent bridal satin powder colors and use them to paint the body and highlight the wings. (Colors with green and blue tinges work well.) Add stronger markings using a finer paintbrush and darker green and blue petal dusts diluted with alcohol.

4 Nontoxic glitter can also be added for extra sparkle. Tiny amounts of nontoxic glue applied to the edges of the wings and body will help to adhere the glitter to the work. Leave the finished piece to dry.

5 The finished dragonfly. Dragonflies work well when added to floral displays, or can be used in various sizes to create a cake design on their own.

Piping bags

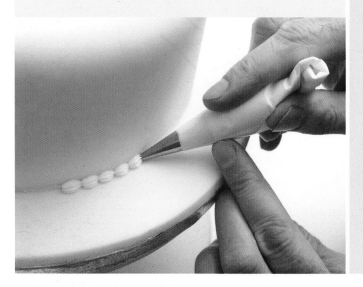

Paper icing bags are far superior to old-fashioned icing syringes. They are inexpensive to make, allowing you to easily create and work with several bags fitted with different-sized tips or filled with different colored icings. It is important to use good quality baking parchment to make strong piping bags. It is obtainable in 15 x 10 in. (38 x 25 cm) sheets, or in rolls. To avoid waste, never make a bag larger than you need for the design you are working on. Shown here are the instructions for making your own bags—but if you decide to cheat you will find that most cake decorating stores sell ready-made paper bags!

Materials
- Baking parchment
- Royal icing

Equipment
- Sharp scissors
- Piping tip
- Palette knife
- Damp cloth

1 Cut a sheet of baking parchment diagonally, see above. This makes two large piping bags. If you require smaller bags, fold and cut the sheet in half prior to cutting diagonally, to create four small piping bags.

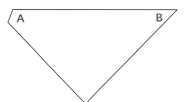

2 Take point A and turn it over in a circle allowing the paper to remain slack. Gradually tighten the paper—bringing point B around—to create a strong, sharp point at the tip of the bag.

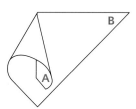

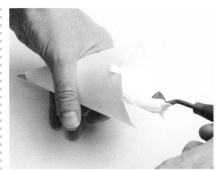

3 Fold over the two points at the top of the bag, then make two small tears or cuts approximately ¼ in. (6 mm) apart and fold the flap down to "lock" the position.

4 **Filling a piping bag**
Cut off the tip of the piping bag using sharp scissors and insert your chosen piping tip. Try not to make the hole in the end too large or you will find that the tip will pop out from the bag when pressure is applied during piping.

5 Hold the piping bag in your left hand. Use a palette knife to fill the bag half to two-thirds full with royal icing. (This will depend upon the consistency of the icing and the size of the tip.) For very fine tips it is best to use only small amounts of icing—large amounts can strain your hand and result in unsteady piping. You will find that the heat of your hand will cause the icing to dry out, very often causing it to break.

6 With your thumb, push down the icing in the bag so that it eases into the piping tip. Next, fold the sides of the bag in toward the center. Keep pushing the icing down into the bag as you then fold over the top of the bag, making it nice and tight.

7 **Holding a piping bag**
Hold the piping bag between your middle and index fingers and push down on the icing with your thumb. Squeeze the icing through the tip and wipe the end with a damp cloth to ensure that the icing forms a clean start when you pipe. Place the pointed end of the tip in position over the work before beginning to push the icing through the bag.

TIPS

- Pressing with and releasing your thumb will cause the icing to flow and then stop. The icing will continue to flow after the pressure has stopped; therefore you must release pressure on the bag before you reach the end of piping a line. You will soon learn how to judge the pressure and movement required to produce the desired effects.

- To pipe a shell, fit a piping bag with a medium grooved (rope or open star) piping tip. Position the pointed end of the tip at the base of the cake. Keep the bag still and push the icing through the tip to start forming a shell. Pull the bag back to form a "tail" to the shell shape. Position the bag to form the next shell so that it just touches or overlaps the first one. Continue around the cake to complete the border.

- Keep wiping the tip from time to time to ensure that the icing produces a good starting point. When not using the filled bag, simply wrap or stand the pointed end of the bag in a damp sponge or cloth.

Piping designs

Once mastered, a piped border or side design can be a very quick and effective method of creating an impressive design on a wedding cake. On these pages are some examples of designs using an assortment of different piping tips. Royal icing or buttercream are best for these designs, but fondant can be used if softened with rose or orange water, or better still clear alcohol.

Small round tip

Snail trail
A fine piped snail trail is wonderful for tidying the join between the base of a cake and board without adding bulk or detracting from other elements of a wedding cake design.

Small round tip

Beads
A series of piped dots or beads can be used in the same way as a snail trail. A slightly damp paintbrush is useful for smoothing down take-off marks on each bead.

Medium rope tip

Small shell border
A small, fine shell border is piped with fine to medium rope tips. This type of border is decorative without overpowering the general design of the cake.

Medium rope tip

Alternating shells
Alternating and linking a series of piped shells using a rope, shell, or star tip can create a very decorative border suitable for the top or bottom edge of a royal-iced or buttercream cake.

Medium leaf tip

Ornate leaves
An ornate border can be created using a medium leaf tip to pipe leaves in repetition. Once the piped leaves have set, frame them with colored icing "beads" using a small round tip. Finally, add dots to the tip of each leaf using another colored icing.

Large open star tip

Ornate shell

A large piped shell border can easily be transformed by adding overpiping or, as pictured here, with a series of dots piped with a small round piping tip.

Medium rope tip

S and C scrolls

This style of border takes a lot of practice and discipline to achieve consistent results. A shaky hand helps to add a rippled texture that complements this style of decoration. Use rope or shell tips for piping S and C scrolls.

Medium open star tip

Small round tip

Stars

Control is needed to pipe stars that are equal in size and height. A fine damp paintbrush is useful for tidying up lift-off marks. Here the stars have been highlighted with small pink dots using a small round piping tip.

Medium leaf tip

Small round tip

Trailing leaves

A fine wavy line piped with a small round piping tip forms the basic trailing stem, onto which a series of equal or graduating sized piped leaves is added using a specialty leaf tip. The icing needs to be a little firmer to produce neat shapes. Fine dotted embroidery style flowers are added to soften the effect (see page 66).

Medium rope tip

Small round tip

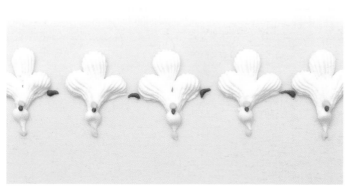

Fleur-de-lys

These are quite simply three shells piped with a rope tip and joined together at the base. Finer colored piped dots and dashes of icing are added for interest and to disguise any bad joins.

Piped embroidery

Use small amounts of piped embroidery at intervals around a cake to fill space without overpowering a floral display, or use embroidery extensively to form the main feature on a cake with a very simple top decoration. Embroidery is best piped onto a cake that has been given at least a day to allow the fondant to "skin over"—however, if you plan to include eyelet holes in the design, these are often best indented into a freshly coated cake. Using a tiny piping tip is not for the beginner.

Materials
- Fondant-coated cake
- Fondant or royal icing
- Petal dusts (optional)
- Clear alcohol (optional)

Equipment
- Modeling stick or knitting needle
- Piping bag and a selection of fine piping tips
- Fine paintbrush

See page 133 for the piped embroidery templates.

Eyelets

1 If you are planning to include eyelet holes in the design, these need to be added while the fondant is still soft—either the same day or the next day at the latest. Indent holes around the cake at intervals using the pointed end of a modeling stick or knitting needle.

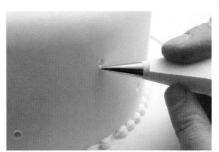

2 Pipe around the holes using white icing in a bag fitted with an extra fine tip. Use a fine, damp paintbrush to blend any significant joins in the design. For large cakes, similar, though less fine, embroidery work can be done with longer tips.

3 Pipe a series of dots around the hole using the same piping bag. Leaves can be represented by piping small teardrop shapes—increase the pressure at the start of the shape and taper off as you reach the tip of each leaf. Again, use a fine, damp brush to tidy up any uneven piping.

Rose design

1 Roses are easy and fairly quick to pipe into an embroidery design. Start by piping a reverse question mark shape. Add three outer petal lines around the center. This will represent a half-rose in a design.

2 Repeat the process to add extra petals and complete a full rose. These tend to fill the design quite quickly. Neaten the edges with a damp brush.

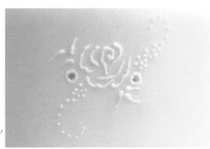

3 Tiny, dotted piped flowers are also great for filling in space and softening embroidery designs. They can take on a simple five-dot flower shape, with an extra one for the center, or extend the dot formations to form lilac-style flowers.

Extra fine round tip

Fine dots

This simple design is guided by a band of ribbon attached to the side of a cake. Tiny dots of icing are formed using an extra fine round tip to build up the design. Pearl dragées are attached with dots of icing at intervals in the design. To add a twist, small dots of luster gel are piped into the design too, which creates a softer effect.

Fine round tip

Extra fine round tip

Dusky rose

Embroidery can be dusted with petal or pearl dusts. For stronger color, use petal dust mixed with clear alcohol. This design uses the techniques described opposite. It is piped using white icing with a fine tip to create the roses and foliage and an extra fine tip for the more delicate dotted flowers. Once the icing has set, add a light dusting of color using assorted petal dusts.

Golden rose

An open rose, piped using a larger tip to create a bolder design. Once the white icing has dried you can gild the design using a mixture of clear alcohol and gold petal dust.

Small round tip

Fine round tip

Extra fine round tip

Sequin and rose

This design is another variation of the rose design illustrated opposite. A fine tip is used to pipe the roses and an extra fine tip for the dotted flowers. The design is painted using diluted mixtures of petal dusts and cocoa butter (see page 82). Cut-out gelatine sequins are added to complete the design (see page 60).

Brush embroidery

Brush embroidery is a technique that allows you to paint pictures with icing. The designs most suitable for this delicate technique tend to be floral—although birds, fish, butterflies, and other insects work very well too. Designs can be copied from bridal lace, dress fabric, floral greeting cards, or freehand designs—the possibilities are endless. The designs work well when executed with white piping on a white coating, creating a delicate texture. White can also be piped onto a colored cake or, for more detail, the design can be painted afterward to create realistic flower designs. If necessary, a small amount of clear piping gel can be added to the icing to slow down the drying process, giving you longer to paint with the icing. Add one teaspoon of piping gel to four tablespoons of royal icing.

Materials
- White fondant or royal icing
- Clear piping gel (optional)
- Water
- Assortment of petal dusts (optional)
- Clear alcohol (optional)

Equipment
- Tracing paper or baking parchment
- Sharp pencil
- Piping bags
- A selection of fine piping tips
- Paintbrushes—assorted sizes

See page 133 for the brush embroidery templates.

1 Trace the design onto a piece of tracing paper or baking parchment with a sharp pencil. Place the tracing paper onto the cake and carefully scribe the design onto the cake coating.

2 Fit a small piping bag with an appropriately sized round tip—this will depend upon the size of the design. (Here, a small tip was used. Small or detailed designs will require an extra fine tip.) Fill the bag with a small amount of icing. Start to pipe the outline of a leaf. Apply quite a bit of pressure to the sections of the leaf that require more icing to fill the shape. Work on one side of the leaf at a time.

3 You will need to use the largest paintbrush that you think the design will take. Dip the brush into water and blot off the excess. Start to carefully brush the icing toward the central vein of the leaf. Try to encourage the icing to take on the direction of the veins on the leaf. Repeat to fill in the other side of the leaf. Extra-fine piped lines can be added to create more emphasized veining, or you could use a fine, damp paintbrush to remove some of the brushed icing in vein form.

4 Pipe the outline of one of the flower petals. A large flower or section of a flower that is in the foreground will need heavier piping, or perhaps even a larger tip, to complete the design. Brush the petals from the edges to the center of the flower, trying to create flowing, petal-like veins.

5 Add a series of dots at the center of the flower to represent the stamens. Use a fine, damp brush to neaten the dots if necessary. Once the design has dried you might decide that you want to use color to highlight and add interest to the design. This can be added using either dry dusting powders to create a soft effect, or by diluting color with alcohol and painting over the icing.

Fine round tip

Small round tip

Almond blossom

A pretty five-petal blossom design created using brushed petals and leaves. To connect the iced flowers together, paint twigs using a fine paintbrush and petal dust diluted with clear alcohol.

Wild rose

Another variation of the wild rose illustrated in steps 1 to 5. The design is piped in white icing and, once dry, painted with petal dusts diluted with clear alcohol.

Viola

It is often best to choose simple, flat-faced flowers for a cake design that is easy to create. These pretty violas are a great example of this.

Lace

Piping lace can be time-consuming but very satisfying; delicate designs can be created on the sides of royal-iced and fondant cakes. It is best to pipe lace using a small piping bag and fine tips. Allow plenty of time to make these small pieces. You can also make larger pieces of filigree to form decorative cake tops—but these can be difficult to transport and keep whole in high humidity. "Antique" lace can be piped with icing colored with a squeezed teabag. Pipe the lace with a shaky hand to create an antique finish.

Materials
- Fondant or royal icing made with fresh egg white
- Piping bags
- Tracing paper
- Wax paper or acetate
- Masking tape

Equipment
- Pencil
- Lace design
- Plastic or nonstick board
- Fine piping tips
- Sable paintbrush

See page 134 for the lace templates.

1 Use a sharp pencil to draw or trace your desired lace design onto a strip of tracing paper. It is best to draw only one or a few pieces so that the lace, when piped, does not differ too much from the original pattern.

2 Tape wax paper or acetate onto a piece of plastic or board with masking tape. Slide the long strip of tracing paper with the lace design under the acetate. Check that you can move the tracing paper along each time you are ready to start piping the next piece of lace.

3 Fit a small piping bag with a fine round tip. If you are using the extra fine tip you will first need to squeeze the icing through a clean nylon sock to remove any difficult grains of sugar that might block the tube. Follow the design slowly and carefully.

TIPS

- It is important that your hands are dry and perspiration-free, as slight moisture can weaken and break the lace.
- Lightly apply shortening to the wax paper. Wipe moisture off with a paper towel. Pipe onto the lightly greased paper. Lace designs will release much easier with less breakage.

4 Continue to pipe each shape, moving the lace design after each piece so that you can pipe the next piece. Add tiny dots to the edges of the lace for extra detail and for added strength. Remove any kinks in the piping with a fine, slightly damp paintbrush.

5 Leave the piped lace to dry for several hours before removing it from the acetate. Use a dry sable brush to help you, or carefully pull the acetate over the edge of the plastic, keeping it tight so that the lace simply eases off.

6 Scribe a scalloped line onto the sides of the cake (see page 40). Pipe two small dots of icing onto the line and carefully attach to the dots. Once the lace is fastened to the cake you can adjust the angle using a fine, dry paintbrush. Continue to add the lace around the cake until completed.

Fine round tip

Ribbon

Attach a band of ribbon around the sides of the cake, then alternately attach lace and dragées to the edge of the ribbon. Paint over each dragée with a mixture of green luster dust and alcohol. Add green and gold highlights to the lace pieces to create a stunning design.

Pink heart vine leaves

A more informal use of piped lace. Prior to removing the lace from the acetate, tinge each piece with a light dusting of pink petal dust. Paint a fine trailing vine and foliage to act as a base to attach the pink heart vine leaves to.

Hearts

To create an open design, try adding piped dots inbetween each heart-shaped lace—this will allow you to use fewer pieces of lace in order to complete the decoration. Add gold highlights to finish the design.

Filigree butterfly

A filigree butterfly can be used to fill space and add interest on a wedding cake. The wings are held in place by a body piped in three sections using a fine round tip. Leave the butterfly white, or paint with diluted petal dusts for a more dramatic effect.

Clay gun techniques

A clay gun can be used successfully with chocolate paste, fondant, gum paste, modeling paste, and marzipan. Whichever type of paste you choose, it will need to be softened a little prior to being used with the clay gun to allow it to be extruded easily. There are several attachments that help to create different effects, including rope, ribbons, tassels, and fine piped lines.

Materials
- Paste (your chosen type)
- Vegetable shortening, or piping gel, work equally well as a softener for fondant or gum paste

Equipment
- Clay gun and a selection of attachments
- Sharp knife

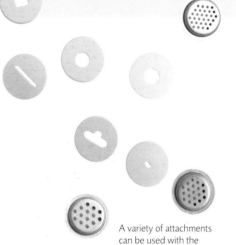

A variety of attachments can be used with the clay gun.

1 First, soften the paste with vegetable shortening and a little water. The paste shown here is a mixture of equal amounts of fondant and gum paste. Knead the shortening into the paste until it feels soft enough to extrude through the clay gun.

2 Unscrew the end of the clay gun and insert the decorative disk attachment required for your design. Screw the end back onto the gun.

3 Roll the softened paste into a sausage shape and insert it into the gun. Try not to overload the gun—this will strain your hand as you are squeezing to extrude the paste. Hold the gun firmly and squeeze the trigger a few times to extrude the paste.

4 Here, one of the rope attachments has been used. To create a twisted rope effect, simply twist the extruded paste back on itself to make the required length.

5 Cut the paste at an angle from the gun. Attach the rope around the base of a cake to create a quick and effective border, connecting the two diagonally cut ends to disguise the join.

Tassel
Use the grass mesh attachment in the clay gun to pipe strands suitable for a tassel. Gather the strands together and tie with a short band of gum paste. Paint as desired. Tassels can work well combined with the rope illustrated opposite.

Curl
Use a ribbon attachment to pipe a single length. Curl accordingly and then flatten with a plastic smoother. Allow to dry, and color as required.

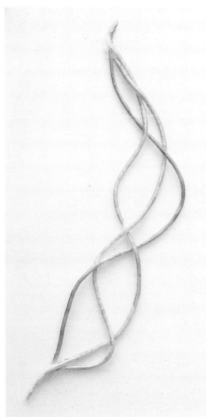

Freestyle
Use a fine single hole attachment to pipe long strands of paste. Twist and tangle several lengths together to form freestyle shapes. Here, the three lengths have been painted different colors to create an eye-catching design.

Loveheart
Use a plain hole attachment to pipe long lengths of paste. Twist two lengths together to form a loose rope effect. Pinch and curl into a heart shape. Use as a side design or form on acetate and allow to dry—the dried heart could form a freestanding cake top design.

The clay gun is a versatile and useful tool for creating paste effects.

Battenburg lace

This technique creates large, strong pieces of decorative filigree lace that can be used around the sides, on the top edge, or even as a central decoration on the cake. The main outline is piped with softened gum paste.

Materials
- Vegetable shortening
- White gum paste
- White royal icing or fondant

Equipment
- Sharp pencil
- Tracing paper
- Masking tape
- Acetate or waxed paper
- Clay gun and ribbon attachment
- Craft knife
- Plastic smoother
- Piping bag fitted with a fine/small round piping tip

See page 134 for the Battenburg lace templates.

1 Trace the lace design using a sharp pencil.

2 Tape the design onto a board with strips of masking tape. Place a sheet of acetate or waxed paper over the top, then smear a light layer of vegetable shortening onto the acetate.

3 Soften some white gum paste with vegetable shortening and a little water, and extrude the paste through a clay gun with a ribbon attachment.

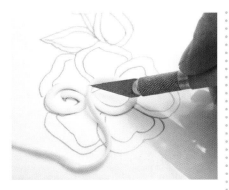

4 Carefully guide the extruded paste around the various sections of the design and use a craft knife to trim the sections if necessary.

5 Use a plastic smoother to flatten the outlined paste design.

6 Fill in the inner parts of the design with icing, using the piping bag and tip. Pipe freehand filigree designs in each section. Leave them to dry, then peel off the Battenburg lace from the acetate and attach it to the cake.

Lace paisley

White gum paste has been used to create a loose paisley design. Extra piped detail has been added using white royal icing in dot and line form. Keep the design white if desired or add gold and green luster definition, diluting the colors with clear alcohol. A single green dragée, overpainted with green luster, is held in place in the center using a dot of piped royal icing.

Curved heart

Form the basic heart outline using extruded white icing. Pipe dots and lines and a section of trellis overpiping within the design. Color as for the paisley, left.

Leaf

A very simple leaf design can work wonderfully as a side decoration on a wedding cake. This time the design is dusted in red, gold, and green food color petal dusts.

Bell

Pipe the heavier outline of a bell with white icing. Add a dotted outline to add strength to the shape, and lines and trellis to add detail. Some gelatine sequins are also attached using dots of royal icing. Dust and paint the shape with gold and blue petal dusts.

Sugar ribbons

You can cut strips of gum paste to create bows and twisted ribbons, or use short pieces of curved sugar ribbon to give the illusion of ribbon insertions through a fondant-coated cake.

Materials
- Gum paste
- Vegetable shortening
- Petal dusts (optional)
- Edible spray varnish (optional)
- Egg white or clear alcohol

Equipment
- Nonstick board and rolling pin
- Long blade
- Craft knife
- Plastic dowel
- Fine tweezers

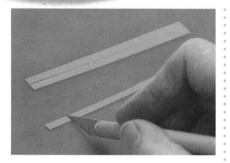

1 To make a ribbon insertion, start by rolling out some well-kneaded gum paste on a nonstick board. Use a long blade to cut "ribbon" strips. Use a sharp craft knife blade to cut $^2/_5$ in. (1 cm) lengths of "ribbon" pieces.

2 Lightly grease a length of plastic dowel with vegetable shortening. Place the cut pieces of sugar ribbon over the dowel to form them into curved shapes. Leave them to dry for several hours. When they are dry, paint or dust the ribbon pieces if desired. Spray or paint the pieces with edible glaze. Leave them to dry again.

3 It is important that the ribbon pieces are pushed into the fondant cake coating while it is still soft. Mark the design onto the side of the cake or plaque. Insert the pieces of sugar ribbon at intervals to complete the design.

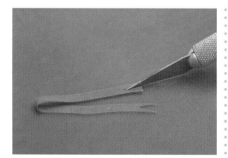

4 You could add sugar bows to complete a pretty side design. Cut a strip of paste as before. Fold the strip in half and then make fine v-shaped cuts in the end of each section.

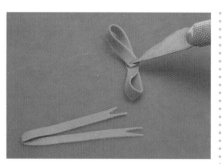

5 Cut another strip of gum paste. Fold each end of the strip into the center to form two loops. Use fresh egg white or clear alcohol to "glue" the two ends in place.

6 Place the looped section of ribbon on top of the tail ends and "glue" it into place. Pinch the center of the ribbon loop with fine tweezers to complete the bow illusion. You can add movement to the tails by twisting them.

Japanese floral

Japanese style flower designs are simple and effective. Cut lengths of sugar ribbon. Curl and assemble the petals using clear alcohol or fresh egg white to hold each section in place. Add a single cut-out blossom (see page 56) at the heart of the "flower." Paint and highlight the design as required.

EMBELLISHMENTS

Twist lengths of sugar ribbon and attach them to the sides of a cake to create a very quick and effective side design. Bows, cut-out birds, or blossoms may all be used to disguise the joins in the scalloped ribbon.

Floral touches

A twisted band of sugar ribbon works well on the sides of the cake, held in place decoratively by birds, butterflies, dragonflies, or in this case tiny punched out blossoms. Painted leaves and dotted flowers can help to soften the design.

Quilled rose

This abstract rose design is made using a length of sugar ribbon curled tightly in an almost quilled manner. The leaves are made in a similar way, pinching the tips to define a leaf shape. Extra punched out blossoms and detailed paintwork complete the design.

Bow

A tied sugar bow is painted with green luster color diluted with clear alcohol. Colorful punched blossoms and painted flowers and leaves are combined to form a very quick and colorful design.

Sugar accents

Wired sugar stars, hearts, feathers, and spirals can be used individually, collectively, or even added to floral displays to create modern cake top designs. These wired pieces are inedible because of the wire content and so should be removed from the cake prior to cutting.

Materials

- Gum paste
- 30-, 28-, or 26-gauge wire
- Petal dust
- 26- or 24-gauge white wire
- Nontoxic glitter

Equipment

- Nonstick board and rolling pin
- Heart-shape cutter
- Medium-sized ball tool
- Flat dusting brush
- Needle-nose pliers

These are the materials and equipment needed for all of the sugar accents.

See page 135 for the sugar accent templates.

Hearts

1 Roll out some well-kneaded gum paste on a nonstick board, leaving a thick ridge in the center to conceal a fine wire. Cut out a heart shape with the cutter.

2 Insert a moistened 30-, 28-, or 26-gauge wire into the thicker, ridged part of the heart shape. Pinch the point of the shape down onto the wire to secure it in place and give it some individuality.

3 Soften the edge of the shape using a medium sized ball tool—work half on your hand and half on the edge of the shape.

4 Leave the shape to dry and then add some colored petal dust, catching the edges of the heart with a flat dusting brush.

Spirals

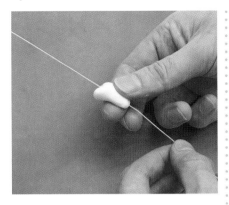

1 Work a piece of well-kneaded gum paste onto a dry 26 or 24-gauge full-length white wire.

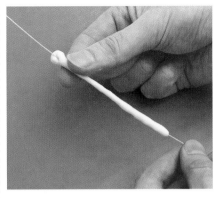

2 Hold the wire firmly with one hand and twist the paste firmly toward the tip of the wire with your other hand. Don't worry about achieving a smooth finish at this stage. Try to taper the thickness of the gum paste so that it is finest at the tip of the wire.

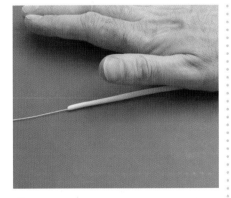

3 Place the coated wire onto a nonstick board and use your hand to roll and smooth along its length.

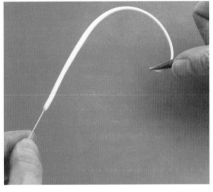

4 Hold the tip of the coated wire with needle-nose pliers and curl it to create the desired spiral effect.

WIRED STARS

You can use a similar method to make wired stars.

ADDING GLITTER

Inedible, nontoxic glitter works well on these wired shapes. Use nontoxic craft glue to stick the glitter to the shape.

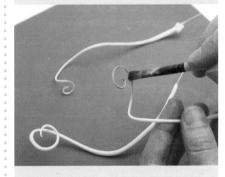

ADDING PETAL DUST

Colored petal dust brushed onto the abstract shapes can help to add interest and blend the shapes into an overall design.

Molds

There are many shapes, sizes, and varieties of commercial molds available to buy, but you may find that making your own helps you to fill the gaps in your collection. Molds can be taken from fresh petals and leaves, pendants, buttons, lace, shells... the list is endless. If you do decide to make your own molds, it is important to use only mold-making mediums that are suitable for use with food items.

Materials

- Silicone putty
- Original for the mold
- Facial cream cleanser
- Leaf or petal

Equipment

- Nonstick plastic board
- Measuring spoon
- Mixing bowl
- Sharp scissors
- Scriber or craft knife

Making a simple mold

1 There are various types of silicone putty available for making molds. The kind shown here is fairly simple to use. It is important to work on a nonstick board, as these materials will stick to anything. Measure equal amounts of each compound using a measuring spoon for accuracy.

2 Mix the two compounds together thoroughly. One compound is a catalyst and once mixed you will have between ten and twenty minutes working time before the mixed medium sets—this often depends upon the weather at the time.

3 Flatten the silicone putty against the board and press the original into the compound. (Here, a seahorse brooch was used.) Leave the putty for ten to twenty minutes to set, then remove the original. You now have a mold of your original object.

Making leaf and petal veiners

1 Mix up some silicone putty, and press the back of a leaf or a petal into it. When the compound has set, peel off the leaf to reveal your leaf veiner mold.

2 Trim away any excess silicone from around the mold with a sharp pair of scissors. Lightly grease the leaf veiner with facial cream cleanser—be careful not to block up the veins with the cream as this will ruin the finished veiner.

3 Mix up another batch of silicone putty and press it firmly on top of the first half of the leaf veiner.

4 Mark the veiner with the leaf or petal name using a scriber or craft knife.

5 When the second half has set pull the two sides apart—and you now have a double-sided leaf veiner.

Insects and birds
A butterfly, bumble bee, dragonfly, or bird can be of great use to the cake decorator because they fill space quickly and easily, complementing many floral displays. The objects pictured here were all made using commercially available sugarcraft molds. A mixture of gum paste and sugarpaste is best to work with these small, fine molds.

White lace
This pretty piece of sugar lace was made with white paste from a commercial mold. The final piece was then highlighted with pearl luster color.

Antique Gold lace
This ornate piece of lace was again made with a commercial mold and white paste but this time was dusted with pearl luster and highlighted with a dilution of clear alcohol and gold petal dust. Dragées and spots of luster gel have been used to add extra detail.

Cocoa painting

It is usual to make sepia tones using a mixture of melted cocoa butter and cocoa powder. But for more delicate designs suitable for wedding cakes, try using petal dusts mixed with melted cocoa butter. Designs can be scribed onto the sides of a cake to use as a guideline when painting, though gradually you will build up enough confidence to paint freestyle flowers and leaves. The fondant surface needs to be left to dry for at least a day so that you have a firm surface to paint on.

Materials
- Cocoa butter
- Petal dusts: light green, dark green, pink, white

Equipment
- Saucer or artist's palette
- Cup or plate warmer
- Sharp knife
- Fine paintbush
- Scriber or craft knife

See page 135 for the cocoa painting templates.

Painting leaves

1 Place a saucer or artist's palette on top of a cup filled with boiled water. (Alternately, you can use a plate warmer.) Grate a small amount of cocoa butter onto the plate using a sharp knife. Mix a little green powder color into some of the melted cocoa butter.

2 Use a fine paintbrush to paint the basic leaf form and stems onto the fondant surface. The design pictured here has been painted free hand—but see also the template on page 135.

3 Next, add a darker green to the melted pale green mixture. Use this to outline and define the leaf shapes. Apply heavier color on one side of the leaf to give the impression of light hitting it from one direction. Blot off the excess paint and then blend the two greens together, using the same brush, to create a more subtle effect. Allow each subsequent layer of colored cocoa butter to dry, otherwise the colors will blend a little too much.

4 Use a scriber or craft knife to etch away fine veins from each leaf. Be careful not to dig the blade into the fondant.

COCOA BUTTER

Cocoa butter is a pure edible vegetable fat that is extracted from the cacao bean and is mixed in varying amounts with cocoa powder to create solid chocolate bars. White chocolate is a mixture of cocoa butter, sugar, and milk solids. It is a very stable fat containing natural antioxidants that prevent rancidity and give it a storage life of two to five years. Its long shelf-life, smooth texture, sweet fragrance, and emollient properties have helped make cocoa butter a popular ingredient in cosmetics and skin care products too! It is sometimes known as theobroma.

Painting petals and flowers

1 With some clean melted cocoa butter and another fine brush, mix some pink and white petal dust together to form a more opaque paint.

2 Paint the basic flower or petal shape. Add more pink petal dust to the mixture where you need more definition and depth in the design. Again, etching can be used to create fine petal veins.

3 Quick, dotted designs quite similar to those used in the section on piped embroidery (see page 66) can be used to great effect with colored cocoa butter. Use a fine brush and a steady hand to create these pretty and quick space-fillers. The cocoa butter designs will turn solid again when dry—however, you must be careful not to leave the cake in a hot room or direct sunlight as this will melt the design!

Lovehearts

This loveheart design could be painted free hand onto the sides of a wedding cake or traced and scribed onto the icing. If the design is to be repeated several times around more than one tier, it is best to keep the detail to a minimum.

Wildflowers

The flowers and leaves in this design are scribed into the icing using the template on page 135. Paint each section in layers as described opposite, this will help to add depth. Etch fine veins in the foliage and flower petals and add dotted flowers to complete the design.

Fantasy bird

Anything can be painted onto a cake if time and patience allows. Human figures, birds, animals, and insects make ideal subjects to create a bold and interesting cake design. This fantasy bird would fill a large area on a cake, which would enable the decorator to use less decoration elsewhere.

Buttercream flip

The buttercream flip technique allows you to create bold images that can be made and frozen well in advance of a celebration. The designs are outlined and then filled in with brightly colored buttercream. The designs can also be highlighted using the cocoa painting technique (see pages 82–83). Pipe small plaques and designs to add to a decorated cake, or you can even coat the whole top surface with one huge buttercream flip.

Materials

- Buttercream: brown, dark pink, green, pale pink
- Cocoa butter
- Petal dusts: pink, purple, eggplant, green
- Cystallized jasmine, violets, and roses (optional)

Equipment

- Template (see page 135 for design)
- Sharp pencil
- Tracing paper
- Acetate or waxed paper
- Masking tape
- Piping bags
- Round piping tips in a range of sizes

See page 135 for the buttercream flip template.

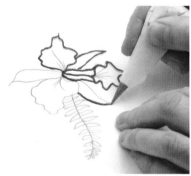

1 Trace the design using a sharp pencil. Place the design onto a cake board or piece of plastic. Place a sheet of acetate or waxed paper over the design and secure it in place with small strips of masking tape. Fit a piping bag with a fine tip and fill the bag with brown buttercream. Carefully pipe around the main outlines of the design (see page 135 for the template).

2 Use a new bag and another fine piping tip to pipe pink detail lines to the floral design. At this stage you might prefer to freeze the design to create a firmer base for the next step. (It is not essential to do so with simple designs.) Fit another bag with a fine piping tip and use green buttercream to fill in each of the fronds of the fern leaf. You will need to increase the pressure with the icing to fill each section.

3 Use a bag fitted with a medium round piping tip to pipe and fill in the main large sections of the flower using a paler pink buttercream. Use a zigzag technique to complete the design.

4 Place another sheet of acetate or waxed paper over the piped design. Carefully smooth over the design using your finger—the heat from your finger will help to soften the icing and blend the piped lines together. Be careful not to press too heavily as this will ruin the design. Next, place the finished design into the freezer for at least half an hour.

5 Remove the design from the freezer. Peel off the top sheet of acetate and then flip the design over. Place it over the cake in the correct position and carefully lower it down onto the cake surface. Use your finger again to smooth over the remaining sheet of acetate and bond the piped design onto the surface of the cake.

6 Peel away the acetate carefully to reveal the finished buttercream flip design. If you are planning to add cocoa painted highlights to the design, refreeze the cake for about ten minutes or so.

7 It is possible to paint melted colored cocoa butter onto the frozen design to add more detail and highlights (see page 83). Take care not to make the melted cocoa butter too hot, as this will melt the buttercream design.

8 Once the design is finished you can add a piped border around the edge of the cake or, for a more fun design, try positioning crystallized jasmine, violets, and roses around the top edge of the cake.

Chocolate decorations

Chocolate work requires very cool conditions and plenty of patience. Take extreme care when melting chocolate; it is very easy to overheat and this makes the chocolate unstable—resulting in pieces that won't set. An electric double-boiler makes it much easier to control the melting process. Melt white chocolate at 84°F (29°C), milk chocolate at 86°F (30°C), and dark chocolate at 89°F (31°C). You can also melt the chocolate above a pan of hot, but not boiling water, or in short bursts in a microwave. Be very careful not to allow steam or water near the melted chocolate as this will cause it to become too thick to work with.

Materials

- Fresh leaves
- Melted chocolate
- White modeling chocolate
- Color dusts (optional)

Equipment

- Brush
- Acetate
- Six-petal blossom cutter
- Dresden tool
- Piping bag

These are the materials and equipment needed for all of the chocolate decorations.

Making chocolate leaves

1 Use only nontoxic forms of plant material for this method—rose, violet, camellia, and mint leaves all work well. It is also important to use fresh plant material that has not been sprayed with harmful insecticides. Wash and dry your foliage, then paint melted chocolate onto the back of the leaf. Place on acetate to dry.

2 When the chocolate has set firmly carefully peel away the real leaf to reveal the chocolate leaf form.

MOLDED CHOCOLATE FLOWERS

These are made using the same technique as marzipan flowers (see page 46). You can buy modeling chocolate from most good cake decorating stores, or make your own by adding liquid glucose to melted chocolate. Melt ³/₄ cup (125 g) of baker's chocolate over a double-boiler, add ¹/₂ cup (100 ml) of warmed liquid glucose and mix well. Wrap in plastic wrap and a plastic bag and leave for at least an hour before handling. White chocolate is more difficult to handle than milk or dark chocolate because it melts more quickly.

White chocolate carnation

1 Roll out some white chocolate onto a nonstick surface. White chocolate tends to melt much faster than milk or dark chocolate so it is important not to overhandle the paste. Cut out a six-petal blossom shape.

2 Work each petal with a stroking action, using the broad end of a Dresden tool. This will thin the petals out and will also create some veins.

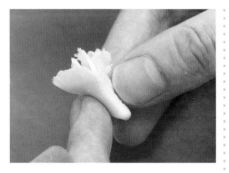

3 Fold the flower shape in half, and then fold again into an "s" shape. Squeeze the shape together to form a tight center for the carnation. Allow this section to rest a little before applying the next layer—especially if you have hot hands.

4 Repeat the process for the next layer. Open up the center of the flower shape and thread it onto the back of the first layer.

5 Repeat with a third layer in the same way as the previous two to complete the carnation. Leave it to allow the chocolate to set. Brush food color dusts onto the edges of the carnation if desired.

Piped chocolate pieces

Fill a piping bag with melted chocolate. Pipe designs onto acetate or silicone paper. Leave to set and then carefully peel away the paper.

Chocolate rose

A hand-molded chocolate rose made using the same technique as for the marzipan rose (see page 46).

Ribbon

Ribbon provides a quick, easy, and very effective way to decorate a cake. Fine bands of ribbon can be used to add an instant splash of dramatic color to a cake design; or they may be used to simply hide joins around the base of a cake. Broader bands of ribbon can even be used to hide dents in the icing. Small ribbon loops be very useful and effective when combined with sugar frills (see page 52) around a cake.

Materials

- Coated cake on a turntable
- Nontoxic glue stick
- Fondant or royal icing
- Clear alcohol or boiled, cooled water
- Fine ribbons
- 28- or 26- gauge wire
- Nile green florist tape

Equipment

- Dresden veining tool or cranked palette knife
- Pearl-head pins
- Fine, sharp scissors

These are the materials and equipment needed for all of the ribbon techniques.

Attaching ribbon to a cake board

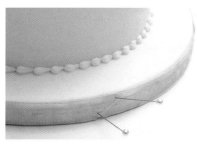

1 It is best to use a nontoxic glue stick around the edge to secure the ribbon. It is tempting to use royal icing to secure the ribbon to a board edge, but the icing tends to ooze through the ribbon and leave a noticeable mark, and often the royal icing will crumble, causing the ribbon to come away from the board.

2 Choose a ribbon deep enough to cover the board edge and the thickness of icing used to cover the board. Trim the excess ribbon using fine, sharp scissors to give a neat finish. Use pins to hold the ribbon in place while the glue is drying, if necessary.

PAPER-COVERED WIRE

This decorative wire is inexpensive and can be bought by the roll. It is intended for gift-wrapping and florist's purposes and is available in an array of colors. If you need an unusual color, white paper-covered wire can be colored by mixing petal dust and clear alcohol on a plate and running the wire through it. Use the wire as a replacement for ribbon loops or braid to add to floral sprays.

Attaching ribbon to the base of a cake

1 First, make some sugar "glue." Soften some rolled fondant with clear alcohol or boiled, cooled water. Use the broad end of a Dresden tool or angled palette knife to blend the two together to create a soft, sticky icing.

2 Place the cake on a turntable. Apply a tiny amount of sugar "glue" to the base of the cake. It is important not to apply dots all around the base of the cake because the icing leaves marks in the ribbon once it has dried. Take a length of fine ribbon and position one end over the "glue." Press the ribbon into place using the broad end of the Dresden tool.

3 Hold the ribbon in place with a pearl-head pin. Move the turntable around as you wrap the ribbon around the base of the cake. Apply a little more "glue" to fasten the two ends of ribbon together. Trim the excess ribbon and secure this end of ribbon with another pin until the glue has dried.

4 Tie a small bow of matching fine ribbon and attach it over the join in the ribbon with another dab of "glue."

BRAIDED RIBBONS

Braided ribbons can be useful if the design requires you to use several colors together. Tie three or more ribbons together at one end—place a weight on the end so that you will be able to use both hands to braid. Attach a braid around the base of the cake as was shown for attaching a single ribbon, or use trails of braided ribbon in among the floral displays.

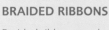

Ribbon loops

1 Fine ribbon looks great when formed and wired into double and treble loops to add to sprays of fresh, silk, or sugar flowers. Loop the ribbon and hold it firmly between your finger and thumb.

2 Add a longer loop of ribbon to create a trail. Bend an open hook in the end of a length of 28- or 26-gauge wire. Place the hook against the ribbon where the loops join. Hold it tightly and then quickly wrap the longer length of wire around it.

3 Tape over the base of the ribbon and down onto the wire with quarter-width florist tape. Cut the longer loop with fine scissors to create two longer trails.

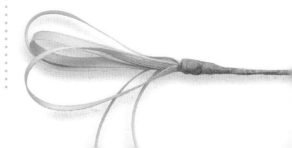

Fresh flowers

Fresh flowers are often used as decoration on wedding and celebration cakes. However, you must take care to use flowers that are not toxic and that have been grown without insecticides. Some companies grow flowers intended for food use, but it is often best to use flowers that you have grown yourself. If you are worried about using fresh flowers against a cake then you may choose to decorate "dummy" cakes (see page 38) and supply separate "cutting" cakes that can be served. This spray features camellia flowers and foliage, roses, and sprigs of rosemary. It is important that the flowers have been conditioned well and given a good drink of water prior to being cut and wired into a spray.

Materials

- 28, 26, and 22-gauge wires
- 5 pink roses
- Nile green florist tape
- 5 camellia leaves
- 3 camellia flowers
- 7 sprigs of rosemary
- Silver-paper-covered wire

Equipment

- Sharp scissors
- Wire cutters
- Tape shredder
- Preparation-wiring single flowers

These are the materials and equipment needed for all of the fresh flower techniques.

Wiring flowers

Push a 22-gauge or stub wire into the stem of a rose, making sure that it is pushed in sufficiently to hold the flower. Tape over with half-width florist tape. (This method is also suitable for other flowers such as orchids, lilies, and carnations.)

Wiring flowers with woody stems

Flowers with woody stems can be wired by twisting a wire tightly around the stem and then simply taping over it with half-width florist tape.

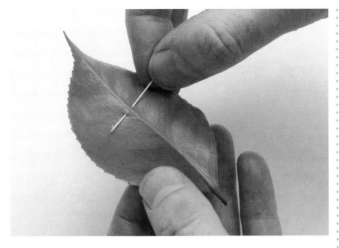

Wiring a single leaf

Use fine wire to thread through the back of the leaf on either side of the central vein. Bend the wire down toward the base and twist the two ends together around the short stem of the leaf. Tape over the stem and down onto the wire with quarter- or half-width florist tape.

Wiring weak-stemmed foliage and flowers

Wind a fine wire around the stem, weaving between the leaves of more fragile plant material. Tape over the base of the stem and wire with quarter- or half-width florist tape. This wiring process will allow you to reshape and bend the stem to create attractive shapes in a spray or bouquet.

Wiring a spray

1 Tape together the three camellia flowers using half-width florist tape. Start with the smallest flower and gradually add a little height to each of the other two. The largest flower will form the focal point of the spray so it needs to be higher than any of the other flowers in the spray. The three stems are joined together to form a handle to the spray. The focal flower should be positioned approximately two-thirds in length from the flowers or foliage at the tip of the spray, with the remaining third of plant materials wired in behind the focal flower.

2 Now add the pink roses, again starting with the smallest flower toward the tip of the spray. Bend and tape each wired stem as you add them to the spray. Cut off any excess wire as you work to reduce the bulk of the handle. Add the wired camellia leaves to fill in the large spaces between the roses and the camellia flowers. Soften the edges and add length to the spray using wired rosemary stems.

3 Add loops and trails of decorative silver-paper-covered wire. Stand back from the spray and take another look at the whole display to check if anything needs repositioning. Keep the spray of flowers in a cool place until it is needed—it is usually best to assemble the flowers the day before or preferably the morning of the wedding to ensure that they are fresh and attractive.

Crystallized flowers

High-quality crystallized flowers can create a very simple, effective decoration for a wedding or celebration cake—you will achieve more variation and individual style by preserving your own selection of flowers and foliage. Whole flowers or individual petals can be used to create a unique design. As with all flowers placed directly next to food it is important to choose only flowers and foliage that are not toxic or that have not been sprayed with insecticides during their growth.

Materials

- Selection of fresh flowers
- Fresh egg white or gum arabic solution
- Superfine sugar
- Boiled sugar solution (optional)

Equipment

- Whisk
- Paintbrush
- Teaspoon
- Sieve, tea-strainer, or fine sugar sifter

Egg-white method

There are two methods for crystallizing flowers. The simplest uses fresh egg white and sugar. Flowers crystallized in this way need to be used fairly soon after being preserved. However, a gum arabic solution and sugar will produce longer-lasting specimens. Some flowers have a very delicate flavor and texture when eaten, while others are used purely to please the eye.

1 Whisk an egg white until just mixed to remove its glutinous consistency but not white and fluffy. Paint egg white all over the petal, flower, or leaf—try not to make it too wet and soggy.

2 Quickly sprinkle the flower, petal, or leaf with superfine sugar, and leave it to dry in a warm place until it becomes crisp to the touch.

SUITABLE FLOWERS AND FOLIAGE FOR CRYSTALLIZING

Roses
Lavender
Violets
Violas (Johnny-jump-ups)
Jasmine
Borage
Scented geraniums
Auriculars
Primroses
Pear blossom
Cherry blossom
Rosemary
Mint
Pinks
Camomile daisies
Cornflowers

Select flowers that you know are not toxic or have not been grown with insecticides. Flowers taken from your own garden or those grown especially for the food industry are best.

GUM ARABIC RECIPE

- ¹/₂ oz (14 g) gum arabic
- ¹/₄ cup (60 ml) warm water

Mix the gum arabic and the water together in a bowl. Place it over a pan of just-boiled water, or in a double-boiler set to a medium heat, and stir until the gum has dissolved. Leave to cool before painting the specimens as described opposite.

If you need the flowers to have a much longer shelf-life, you will need to paint them with the gum arabic solution, allow them to dry, and then paint them with a boiled, cooled sugar solution. Boil 4 oz (113 g) sugar with ¹/₄ cup (60 ml) water until it reaches a temperature of 150°F (80°C). When cool, brush it onto the petals and then quickly sprinkle or sieve superfine sugar over the top.

You might prefer to buy good quality ready-made crystallized flowers. Although these can be expensive to buy, they save a lot of time and have a much longer shelf-life than homemade flowers.

Sugar flowers

There is something very special about a wedding cake decorated with beautiful hand-made sugar flowers. The flower modeling skills in this chapter give a comprehensive insight into sugar flower making that will prove indispensable to both the novice and the more experienced cake decorator, and the particular flowers featured are some of the most popular requested by brides for wedding cakes and arrangements.

Sugar flower modeling

The paste used to make sugar flowers contains gum tragacanth, which gives it stretch and strength, and allows it to be rolled out very thinly if necessary. Although gum paste is technically edible it doesn't taste very good and, because of the extensive use of wire, florist tape, stamens, and thread used in the construction of sugar flowers they are usually considered nonedible and are removed from the cake prior to cutting. The flowers do, however, make a wonderful keepsake.

Materials
- White vegetable shortening
- Gum paste
- Fresh egg white
- Paper-covered wires
- Stamens
- Nontoxic glue
- Petal dusts
- Florist tape
- Edible food glaze

These are the materials and equipment needed for all of the sugar flower modeling techniques.

Equipment
- Nonstick board and rolling pin
- Cornstarch dusting bag
- Sharp scissors
- Flower and leaf cutters
- Dowels
- Plain-edged cutting wheel
- Petal and leaf veiners
- Ball tools
- Silk veining tool
- Dresden veining tool
- Paintbrushes
- Craft knife
- Fine-angled tweezers
- Pliers

Working with gum paste

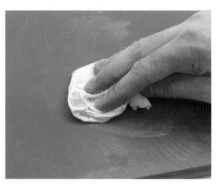

1 Lightly grease the work board with white vegetable shortening and then wipe over and clean it off with paper towel. This will keep the board conditioned and will also help to release the gum paste from the board. You will need to keep reapplying the grease from time to time, otherwise you will find that the paste sometimes sticks to the board especially when it is rolled very finely. The shortening also helps to remove any color left over from previous flower-making sessions.

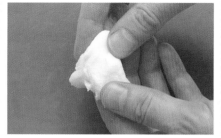

2 This piece of gum paste is taken from the main batch. At this stage the paste is quite firm and often slightly crumbly too. Dust cornstarch on your fingers to keep them from sticking to the paste.

3 Knead the paste firmly between your fingers and thumbs to make it more pliable. This process also helps to warm the gum tragacanth in the paste, giving it more stretch and malleability. The paste will make a clicking sound in your fingers as it is kneaded—this is a sign that it is kneaded sufficiently and ready to use.

4 Knead a tiny amount of white vegetable shortening into the paste if it feels too sticky—however, take care not to add too much as this will result in a "shorter" paste and will also slow down the drying process. Fresh egg white can be added to soften the paste if it feels too dry. Wrap the paste tightly in a plastic bag when not in use.

Simple bud shape

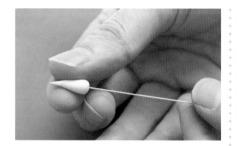

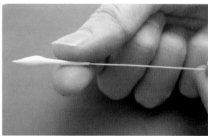

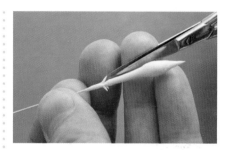

1 Break off a small piece of gum paste and roll it firmly against your palm to form a smooth ball. Next, form the ball into a cone shape, creating a sharp point. Moisten a wire with fresh egg white and insert into the base of the cone. Some larger buds might require a hook in the end of the wire to secure them in place.

2 Next, work the base of the cone firmly between your finger and thumb to create an elongated "neck" to the bud shape—you might need to use a small amount of cornstarch. Continue to work the paste down onto the wire to create a longer, more elegant shape if required—this will depend on the type of bud you are making.

3 At this stage you might need to add a quick, snipped calyx with a pair of small, sharp scissors. Here, five snips have been added and then pinched slightly between finger and thumb to soften the effect slightly.

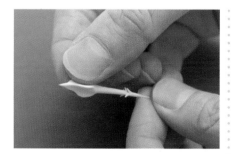

4 To create an unfurled petal effect on a bud, divide the bud using a craft knife or—as illustrated above—simply pinch some petals from the main body of the bud using your finger and thumb.

5 Twist the petals tightly using your fingers and thumb to create a slightly spiraled effect. Support the neck of the bud with your other hand.

6 Continue to twist the bud into shape and then pinch the tip to tidy up the shape. Keep the neck of the bud straight, or carefully create an elegant curve, supporting the wire inside the bud.

Simple cutter flower

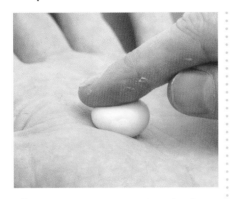

1 Grease the board. Roll a ball of well-kneaded gum paste firmly between your palms to make it smooth. Apply pressure with your index finger to one side of the paste to start to work it into a cone shape. You might need a light dusting of cornstarch at this stage.

2 Continue to work the paste against your hand or the work board to create a sharp, pointed cone shape. Gradually apply more pressure and continue to roll the long section of the cone shape to create a more elongated shape.

3 Smooth the neck of the flower between your palms using a rolling action—this can also be used to give a more elegant shape to the neck.

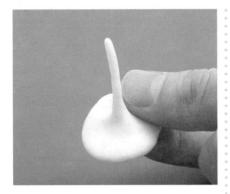

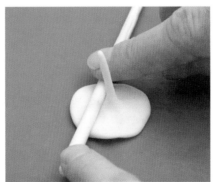

4 Next, pinch the base of the shape between your fingers and thumbs to create a slight "hat" shape, or stem. Continue to pinch the brim of the "hat" to thin it out slightly. Keep pinching around the base of the stem to create a fine neck to the flower—this will make it easier to fit the flower cutter over the neck of the flower.

5 Place the shape against the work board and, using a fine rolling pin or dowel, roll out the "brim" of the hat shape to thin it evenly. Lightly dust the board with cornstarch. Lift up the "brim," and place it on top of the cornstarch so that it will move more easily when the flower shape is cut out.

6 Carefully place your chosen flower cutter over the neck of the flower and press it firmly against the rolled-out paste on the board. Quickly cut out the flower shape. Pick up the cutter with the flower still stuck in it and quickly rub your thumb over the edge of the cutter to create a cleaner cut and remove any ragged edges on the flower.

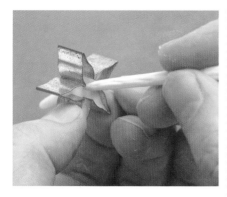

7 Using the pointed end of a dowel or modeling tool, push the flower shape out of the cutter—it is best to push from the cut, flat side of the flower.

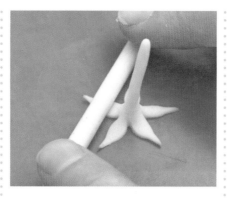

8 Place the flower shape flat side down against the work board. Use a fine rolling pin or dowel to elongate each petal evenly to create a finer flower shape.

9 Open up the center of the flower using the pointed end of a dowel or modeling tool—you might require a light dusting of cornstarch on the tool prior to this stage.

10 Give a bit of "attitude" to the flower petals by pinching the tips of each between your finger and thumb.

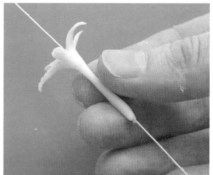

11 Moisten the end of a hooked wire or a set of wired stamens with fresh egg white and thread through the center of the flower (see page 101). You might need to twist the wire to help it thread through the flower throat.

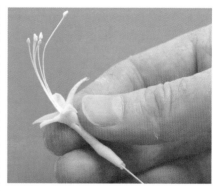

12 Pinch the flower shape behind the petals to secure it onto the hook or stamen center. Work the paste between your finger and thumb to create a finer neck, if required. Add a snipped calyx if you like.

Stamens

These may be added one by one to the center of a flower or glued together and secured onto a wire using hi-tack nontoxic craft glue—this forms a good, strong bond and keeps the stamens from falling out of the flower at a later stage. This technique may be used for simple flowers or more complex centers—for example, the open rose on page 110.

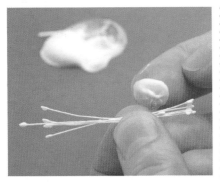

1 Take five stamens, plus an extra one to represent the pistil. Hold them tightly at one end and apply a small amount of hi-tack nontoxic glue to bond them together at the base. Squeeze the glue firmly to secure and create a slightly flattened surface.

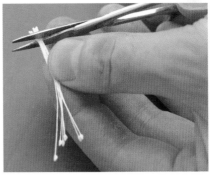

2 Allow the glue to set—it should only be a matter of minutes—and then cut off the tips of the stamens from the glued end.

QUICK ORNAMENTAL GRASS

Apply a thin layer of gum paste onto the end of a dry 33-gauge wire. Smooth the surface between your palms and then texture the entire surface using a fine pair of scissors. Curve gently and color as required.

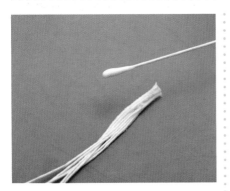

3 Apply a little more glue to the end of a wire and place it down against the stamens.

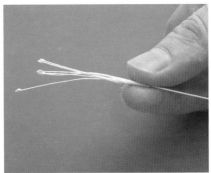

4 Pick up the stamens and the wire and wrap them around the tip of the wire, pinching firmly to secure them in place.

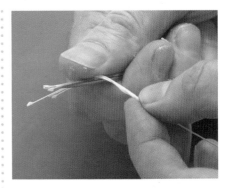

5 Allow them to set, and then carefully curve the stamens against a pair of scissor blades to create a gently curved effect. Dust the stamens if desired prior to adding to the flower.

Wiring a petal or leaf

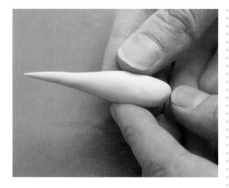

1 Form a ball of well-kneaded gum paste into a long teardrop shape.

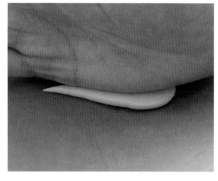

2 Place the shape against the work board and flatten slightly using the side of your hand.

3 Thin out the paste using a fine rolling pin or dowel.

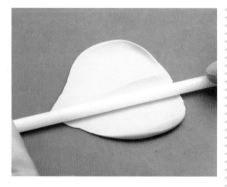

4 Roll the paste away from you, leave a thick ridge area through the center, and then roll the paste toward you. Keep rolling the paste until you have the required leaf/petal thickness, while maintaining the central ridge.

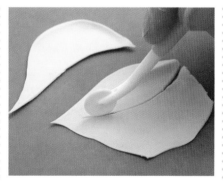

5 Cut out the leaf or petal shape using a craft knife, a cutting wheel, or your chosen flower/leaf cutter.

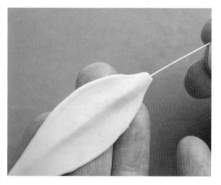

6 Moisten the end of a wire and carefully insert it into the base of the thick ridge. Support the ridge firmly with your finger and thumb to prevent the wire from escaping. The wire may be inserted from a quarter to two-thirds of the way into the ridge to give the shape the support it requires.

SERRATED OR DOUBLE-FRILLED EDGE

A serrated edge can be created quickly using the broad end of a Dresden veining tool. Place the leaf or petal against the board and press the tool into the edge of the shape, pulling it down and out against the board. Repeat around the shape to create an interesting edge effect.

Veining

1 Veins may be added to sugar flowers and leaves using real petals or the silicone rubber veiners that are available from specialist cake decorating stores. The one shown here is double-sided to create a veining effect on both sides of the leaf.

2 Place the leaf into the veiner, lining up the tip and the wire with the central vein of the veiner.

3 Place the other side on top of the leaf and press firmly to emboss the leaf veining successfully.

4 Pinch the leaf from the base, following through to the tip, to accentuate the central vein and give the leaf more interest and movement. Allow the leaf to dry over a slightly curved surface or on crumpled paper towel.

SOFTENING A PETAL EDGE

Place the cut-out petal onto a firm foam pad or your palm. Use a ball tool to thin and soften the edges, or apply a little more pressure to create a soft, frilly edge. A rolling motion can be used or the tool may simply be rubbed against the edge of the petal to create slightly different effects.

CURLED EDGES

The edge of a petal can be curled using your fingers or with a toothpick, paintbrush handle, or modeling tool.

CUPPING A PETAL

Place the petal in your palm or on the pad and use a rolling motion with a ball tool at the center of the petal to form the petal into a cupped shape—this is good for many flowers including roses, peonies, and camellias.

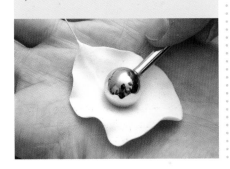

Drying a petal over a former

Cut a strip of paper towel using sharp kitchen scissors. Twist the paper back onto itself and then tie into a loop to make a convenient petal former. Rest the cupped petal in the center of the loop with the curved petal edges over the side of the form. This form allows the petal to breathe and the paste to dry a little faster than if it is placed in a commercial flower-former.

Freestyle veining and frilling

1 A silk veining tool can be useful for many flowers where a light, fairly random veined surface is required. Roll the veined end of the tool against the surface of the petal, working in a fan-shaped formation.

2 Increase the pressure at the edge of the petal using the silk veining tool or even a toothpick or paintbrush handle to create a more frilled, decorative edge. A light dusting of cornstarch may be needed to prevent the tool sticking to the sugar.

3 To make the central vein, place the petal or leaf onto a foam pad. Use the fine end of the Dresden tool to simply draw a line down the center. Pick up the petal or leaf and pinch from the base to the tip to accentuate the vein.

Creating depth

COLORING EFFECTS

Sugar flowers and foliage can be brought to life by dusting them with food-color dusting powders. Coloring can be used lightly to create delicate effects or in layers to produce more realistic, intense coloring. It is often best to use the colors in layers, gradually building up to create depth and character. It is best to have several brushes and to keep certain brushes for particular colors so that you don't mix them.

1 Depth can be achieved easily by dusting heavily at the base of a petal using a flat, bristled paintbrush and a strong, bold color.

2 Gradually work the color toward the center and edges of the petal so that the color gradually fades toward the edge.

3 Depth can also be added at the center of a flower to create a strong focal area. Here a rose is being dusted intensely at the center, which helps to create a bolder, eye-catching flower color.

Paper towel
Use a paper towel to dab off excess dusting powder prior to applying it to the flower, otherwise you will overload the flower with coloring, making the color difficult to control.

Dusting a leaf

1 Catching the edge with dark red or eggplant coloring helps to give a leaf a natural finish. Here the color has been used on the edge, and depth has been created by adding color at the base of the leaf, too.

2 Use green dusting powders in layers to create realistic foliage effects. A light layer of forest green from the base fading toward the edge, but focusing on the central vein, helps to create depth.

3 Over-dust with a lighter green and then blend the layers together, scrubbing the color into the surface of the leaf. Shake off any excess color.

4 Use the color left on the brush to drag across the raised veins on the back of the leaf. Remember, the back of a leaf is usually much paler than the upper surface.

Steaming and glazing

1 The steam from a kettle or clothes steamer can be used to "set" the dry dusting colors onto a flower or leaf and give the finished article a slight sheen or glossy finish. Take care not to steam too heavily, as this can dissolve too much of the flower!

2 You can buy edible food glaze from specialty cake decorating stores. This is simply sprayed onto a leaf lightly or heavily depending upon the degree of glaze you require. It is best to use these sprays in a well-ventilated area.

GENTLER EFFECTS

Catch the edges gently using a flat brush and dragging the bristles over the edge of each petal in turn to create intense color on the edges, fading the color a little in the direction of the base of the flower. White petal dust can be added to the powder colors if you want to calm down the color and create a paler version.

SPOTS AND MARKINGS

Liquid food colors or diluted paste or powder colors mixed with alcohol can be used to paint realistic markings and effects onto both petals and leaves. It is best to use a fine paintbrush for most flowers.

Sugar flower arrangements

Making sugar flower sprays and arrangements is a very satisfying process but it takes practice to perfect. You can follow conventional florist techniques as a guideline. However, sugar flowers often need to be given an extra "twist" to create a more lifelike result. Sugar flowers are much more fragile than fresh flowers and so extreme care must be taken when assembling corsages, sprays, bouquets, or arrangements. Sprays of sugar flowers contain so many inedible items—wires, stamens, ribbons, and so on—that it is very important that the flowers are removed from the cake prior to it being cut.

Materials

- Sugar flowers: Ruscus (page 124), roses and rosebuds (pages 112 to 115), ivy (page 125)
- Nile green florist tape
- Fine crimped wire with pearls threaded at intervals
- Ribbon
- Florists' foam
- Sugar accents (page 78)
- Ribbon loops (page 88)
- Posy pick
- Plastic, vase, candle holder, or small cake board
- Paper-covered wire

Equipment

- Needle-nose pliers
- Wire cutters or strong florists' scissors

These are the materials and equipment needed for all of the sugar flower arrangements.

Wiring a sugar flower bouquet

1 One florists' guideline that you might find useful as a starting point is to think of a spray or bouquet in thirds. The spray should measure two-thirds from its tip to the focal point, with the remaining third being from the focal point to the top of the spray. Here, two stems of Ruscus were formed so that one measures two thirds of the length of the bouquet and the other forms the remaining third.

2 Bend the ends of both Ruscus stems at 90-degree angles using needle-nose pliers. Tape the two stems together using half-width florist tape. The two stems will form a "handle" to the bouquet, which makes adding the remaining flowers and foliage fairly straightforward. Continue to add the remaining stems of Ruscus to form more of the outline of the bouquet.

3 Next add the focal flower—in this instance the largest rose is used as the focal point and needs to stand slightly higher than any of the other flowers that are added subsequently.

4 Add the remaining smaller roses and rosebuds around the focal flower. Use the buds at the very edges of the spray. Trim off any excess wires if the handle of the bouquet starts to get too bulky.

Arranging sugar flowers in florists' foam

This process tends to be easier than wiring a bouquet. The flowers and foliage are simply pushed into florists' foam (or marzipan). If you make a mistake you will find it easy to pull out and rearrange the components.

1 Florists' foam is great for arranging sugar flowers into. However, this medium is not edible, so you will need to secure it onto a piece of plastic, a vase, a candle holder, or a small cake board to separate it from the surface of the cake. Bend a hook in the ends of the flowers and foliage before inserting them into the foam—this hook adds extra support. Squeeze the foam around the stem if more support is needed.

5 Add "filler" flowers to fill in the remaining gaps, or for a quicker result use wired loops of ribbon, as shown here. Beads or pearls strung together on fine crimped wire can be added for a little more interest. Wind the pearls carefully through the stems of the flowers and foliage.

6 Add a double trail of ribbon to complete the bouquet. Tape over the handle of the spray with full-width florist tape to create a neat finish. Use needle-nose pliers to rearrange any components to create a prettier and more relaxed overall effect. Use a posy pick to hold the flowers in position on the finished cake.

2 Use trailing stems of ivy to add length and height to the arrangement. Use needle-nose pliers to push stems into tight spaces in an arrangement.

3 Add stems of Ruscus to fill out the sides of the arrangement. Twisted sugar accents can be added for extra interest. Refine the shape of the arrangement and add a few twists of paper-covered wire. Curl the ends to create more impact. Add extra flowers, foliage, or ribbon at the back of the arrangement to hide the mechanics.

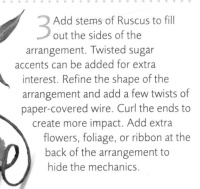

Fantasy blossom

Here are two types of very simple fantasy "filler" flowers that can be made using the same five-petal blossom cutter set. These are wonderful for the complete novice cake decorator.

Trailing blossom

1 Attaching the bud
Bend a hook in the end of a 33-gauge white wire. Attach a tiny cone of white gum paste onto the hook to represent a bud. Roll out some more white gum paste thinly and cut out blossom petals using the three sizes of blossom cutter, alternatively you can use the templates on page 136.

2 Shaping the petals
Place the blossoms on a foam pad and quickly hollow them out using the small ball tool.

3 Assembling the blossom
Attach a tiny ball of white paste a little way down the stem. Moisten the ball with egg white and thread a small blossom onto the wire so that it sits tightly against the gum paste at the top. Add blossoms down the stem, gradually increasing the size of the blossoms as you work, to create pretty trailing stems. Allow the gum paste to dry and brush the petals with petal dust to add color.

Attach a cone of gum paste to the hook (1).

Cut out blossoms using three sizes of cutter (1).

Thread a blossom onto the wire (3).

Make sure the blossom sits tightly against the gum paste (3).

Dust the blossoms with petal dust (3).

Filler blossom

1 Attaching the buds
Cut short lengths of 33-gauge wire. Bend a hook in the end of each. Attach a tiny ball of white gum paste onto the end of each for the flower centers. Allow the centers to dry.

2 Assembling the blossoms
Cut out several blossom shapes using the three sizes of cutter and hollow them out using the small ball tool. Moisten the dried flower center at the base with fresh egg white and thread a blossom onto it. Allow to dry before using a brush to color the blossoms with petal dust.

3 Making clusters of stems
Model small cone shapes onto 33-gauge wire to represent buds. Tape groups of stems into small clusters.

Materials
- Gum paste: white
- 33-gauge white wire
- Fresh egg white
- Petal dust: assorted colors

Equipment
- Five-petal plunger blossom cutters (set of three)
- Foam pad
- Needle-nose pliers (optional)
- Small ball tool
- Flat dusting brush

See page 136 for the fantasy blossom templates.

Lily-of-the-valley

This is a quick and simple version of lily-of-the-valley that is a really useful starting point for the beginning cake decorator. The stems can look great in bunches on a cake or as a filler flower alongside other, larger flowers in sprays and bouquets. In reality the flowers have six petals but as this is a quick method—these only have five.

Materials
- Gum paste: white
- 33- and 24-gauge white wires
- Nile green florist tape
- Petal dust: vine green, foliage, and white

Equipment
- Tiny five-petal plunger blossom cutter
- Needle-nose pliers
- Pointed modeling tool

See page 136 for the lily-of-the-valley templates.

The buds and flowers

1 Making the buds
The buds are very simple—you could make up stems consisting entirely of buds for a very quick and effective filler. Cut several very short lengths of 33-gauge white wire. Bend a hook in the end of each with the needle-nose pliers. Roll lots of balls of white gum paste in gradated sizes. Insert a hooked wire into each ball and reshape if necessary. Allow the buds to dry.

2 Making the flowers
Cut very short lengths of 33-gauge white wire and bend a hook in the end of each. Roll out a small amount of white gum paste and cut a flower shape using the plunger blossom cutter or the templates on page 136. Quickly roll a ball of white paste and place the soft blossom shape onto the ball—if both pieces of paste are still fresh they will stick together without the need for fresh egg white.

3 Finishing the flowers
Embed the blossom into the ball of paste using the pointed end of the modeling tool, which should also help to create a hollowed-out finish. Moisten a hooked wire and thread it through the center of the flower. Repeat to make between five and seven flowers for each stem. Allow the flowers to dry.

Coloring and assembly

4 Adding flowers to stems
Start by taping a tiny bud onto the end of a 24-gauge wire using quarter-width Nile green florist tape. Continue adding the buds, gradating the size as you add them to the stem—add between five and nine buds per stem. Next, introduce the flowers.

5 Curling the stems
Use the needle-nose pliers to curl the stem of each flower and bud so that the heads curve downward.

6 Finishing touches
Dust the main stem and each of the shorter ones with white and vine green petal dust. Add some to the smaller buds, gradually decreasing the amount as you approach the flowers. Tinge the base of the main stem with foliage green petal dust.

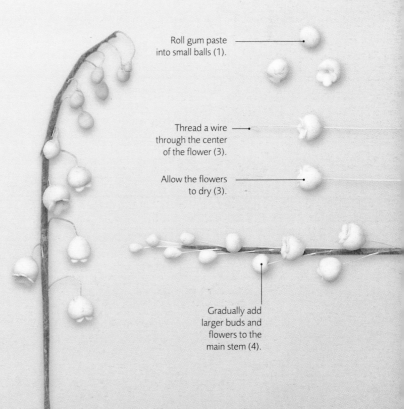

Roll gum paste into small balls (1).

Thread a wire through the center of the flower (3).

Allow the flowers to dry (3).

Gradually add larger buds and flowers to the main stem (4).

Open rose

Open roses are easier to make than the more formal standard rose (see page 112). The number and size of petals vary between the varieties. Wiring each of the petals helps to create a more interesting flower.

The stamens

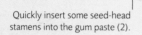

Attach a tiny amount of gum paste onto the hook of wire (1).

Quickly insert some seed-head stamens into the gum paste (2).

Divide more stamens into groups and line up their tips (3).

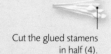

Cut the glued stamens in half (4).

Dust the stamen center with petal dust (5).

1 Shaping the stamens
Cut a half-length of 26-gauge white wire. Bend a small, open loop in one end of the wire using needle-nose pliers. Bend the loop back against the main length of wire. Hold the hook at the center with pliers and bend it to form a "ski pole" shape. Attach a small amount of pale green gum paste onto the hook.

2 Finishing the stamens
Cut some short lengths of seed-head stamens and quickly insert into the soft paste. Allow the stamens to dry.

3 Preparing the flower center
The number of stamens you will need to complete the center for the flower will depend on the size of the flower you are making. Divide the stamens into smaller groups. Line up their tips so that they are evenly positioned. Bond each group together at the center using nontoxic craft glue. Squeeze the glue into the strands of the stamens and flatten them as you work. Leave a short length of stamen at either end unglued. Allow the groups of stamens to dry for a few minutes.

4 Assembling the center
Cut the stamens in half and trim away the excess to leave short lengths. Attach these small groups around the dried flower center using nontoxic craft glue. Allow it to dry and then curl the stamens using tweezers to create a more open, relaxed center.

5 Coloring the stamens
Dust the stamen center and the length of the stamens with vine green petal dust. Mix together lemon and primrose petal dusts and color the tips of the stamens. Add tinges of nut brown and eggplant to the tips if desired.

Materials
- 30-, 28-, and 26-gauge white wire
- Gum paste: white and pale green
- Nile green florist tape
- Nontoxic craft glue
- Petal dust: vine green, white, primrose, lemon, plum, nut brown, and eggplant

Equipment
- Needle-nose pliers
- Sharp curved scissors
- Small seed-head stamens
- Tweezers
- Flat dusting brush
- Rose petal cutters
- Small rose or Christmas rose petal veiner (optional)
- Large ball tool
- Paper towel
- Rose calyx cutters

See page 136 for the open rose templates.

The petals

6 Cutting the petals
Use three sizes of rose petal cutters to create the petals for the open rose (see page 136 for petal templates). The quantity is not too important—however, it is often wise to make more petals than you think you will need, just in case you decide to create a fuller flower. Use white gum paste or add a touch of color if desired—the flower pictured has a touch of vine green added to it to create a warmer base color. Roll out some paste leaving a thick ridge for the wire. Cut out the petal using one of the rose petal cutters

7 Wiring and veining
Insert a moistened wire (the gauge will depend on the size of the petal) into the thick part of each petal. Soften the edge of the petals and then vein them using a rose or Christmas rose petal veiner.

8 Shaping the petals
Hollow out the center of each petal using a large ball tool or simply by rubbing the center of the petal with your fingers and thumb. Curl back the edges of the petal and allow them to dry, supported by a ring of paper towel (see page 102). Repeat to make lots of petals in all three sizes. Some of the smallest petals can be snipped into with curved scissors to create interesting, not-quite-formed petal shapes.

Insert a moistened wire into the thick part of each petal (7).

Soften the edges of the petals (7).

Assembly

9 Putting it all together
Start by taping a few of the not-quite-formed small petals tightly around the stamens. Continue to add the other petals, gradually increasing the petals in size as you work.

10 Adding color
Dust at the base of each petal with a light mixture of primrose, vine green, and white petal dust—this will help to give the rose a natural "glow." Catch the edges lightly with plum and white petal dust mixed together.

11 Finishing
Add a calyx as described on page 114, and follow the instructions for making rose leaves and buds on pages 113 and 115.

Hollow out the center of each petal (8).

Snip into some of the smaller petals to make interesting semi-formed petal shapes (8).

Formal rose

Roses are still the most popular bridal flower for wedding cakes. However, they can prove to be difficult for both the beginning and experienced decorator to produce consistently. There are several petal combinations for creating realistic roses—this is one of the simpler variations.

Materials

- Gum paste: white and mid green
- 30-,28-, 26-, and 18-gauge white wires
- Petal dust: primrose, white, vine green, plum, forest green, foliage, and eggplant
- Fresh egg white
- Nile green florist tape
- Half-glaze or edible spray varnish

Equipment

- Rose petal cutters
- Foam pad
- Metal ball tool
- Smooth ceramic tool
- Small paintbrush
- Rose calyx cutter
- Nonstick board
- Fine, curved scissors (optional)
- Grooved board (optional)
- Rose leaf cutters
- Rose leaf veiner or fresh rose leaf
- Flat dusting brush

See page 136 for the formal rose templates.

Cone center and first layer

1 Starting the rose
Tape over a half to three-quarter length of 18-gauge wire with half-width Nile green florist tape. Bend a large open hook in the end using needle-nose pliers. Form a ball of well-kneaded white gum paste into a cone shape measuring about two-thirds of the length of the smallest rose-petal cutter you are planning to use.

2 Forming the cone
Moisten the hook and insert into the rounded base of the cone. Push the hook into most of the length of the cone. Pinch the base of the paste onto the wire to secure the two together. Allow to dry for as long as possible.

3 Coloring the paste
This rose has been made with white gum paste, but you could mix any color. It is best to color the paste for a strongly colored rose slightly paler than you require the finished rose to be—this allows you to add more depth with layers of petal dust later on. Color more paste than you require, as it can be tricky rematching a depth of color at a later stage if you run out.

Cut out a petal using the small rose petal cutter (4).

Soften the petal edges (4).

Cut out some larger petals (8).

Hollow out the center of the larger petals (8).

Form a cone shape on a wire with gum paste (2).

Add the first petal to the cone and tuck the left-hand side in tightly to begin to create a spiral effect (5).

Add a further two petals and interlink them to create an "S"-shaped spiral (6).

Add the petals layer-by-layer and then tighten them around the bud continuing the "S"-shape formation (7).

The bud

4 Forming a petal
Roll out some gum paste fairly thinly. Cut out one petal using the smaller of the two rose petal cutters you are planning to use (see templates on page 136). Place the petal on a foam pad and soften the edges using a metal ball tool, working half on the edge of the petal and half on the pad and using a rolling action. Try not to frill the edges—you are only taking away the cut edge of the petal.

5 Adding the first petal
Place this first petal against the dried cone using a little fresh egg white to help stick it in place. Position it quite high against the cone so that you have enough of the petal to curl tightly and create a spiral effect around the cone. Tuck in the left-hand edge of the petal and spiral the petal around to form a neat point. The cone should not be visible.

6 Making more petals
Roll out some more gum paste and cut out two petals using the same sized cutter as before. Soften the edges and then moisten them very lightly with fresh egg white. Place the first petal over the join in the petal on the cone. Stick down the left-hand edge and tuck the next petal underneath. Close the first petal over the top of the second so that you have created an "S"-shaped spiral. If you are intending to make a bud you will need to curl the side edges of these petals back at this stage and add a calyx. Otherwise keep the petals tightly together, ready to add the next layer.

7 Building up the bloom
These are a repeat of the second layer, creating an "S"-shaped spiral with each pair of petals. You might not need all six layers—you will gradually get a feel for how many petals you need to add to create an attractive rose. Gradually open up the edges of the petals as you work toward the sixth layer. You might decide to stop after a few layers to create a more open bud, or continue to the next stage to create what is termed a "half" rose.

Half rose stage

8 Forming the petals
Roll out more gum paste and cut out three petals, using the slightly larger rose petal cutter. Soften the edges as before. This time, start to hollow out the center of each petal using a large ball tool or by simply rubbing the petal with your thumb.

9 Attaching the petals
Moisten the base of each petal and create a "V" shape. Attach the petals to the rose as before, trying to place each petal over a join in the previous layer. Pinch either side of each petal at the base as you attach it, so that it retains its cupped shape. Curl back the edges using a smooth ceramic tool, or just your fingers, to create more movement in the petal edges.

Full rose stage

10 Adding the last petals
Roll out some more white gum paste and cut out five to eight petals, using the same large cutter as for the previous layer. Soften and cup as before. Attach the petals so that they cover joins in the half rose layer. It is best to add petals opposite each other to create the correct overlapped finish. Keep cupping the petals and curling back the edges as you work. At this stage you might need to hang the flower upside down to allow the petals to firm up before curling them back into their final position.

...or for a fully open flower, continue to add a further three petals using a larger petal size (8).

You could stop after several layers to create an open bud... (7).

Add a further three petals, each over a join in the previous layer. As the rose widens out, curl back the edges of the petals to create movement (9).

Continue to add petals opposite each other to create the correct finish (10).

Cut out the calyx shape using
a rose calyx cutter (13).

Hollow out each sepal
using a ball tool (14).

Snip into the edges of the
calyx with fine scissors (14).

Coloring

11 Coloring the petals
Mix together white, primrose, and vine green petal dusts. Using a small paintbrush, add a "glow" at the base of each petal, back and front—there will be some petals that you will not be able to get at with a brush but don't worry about these! Next, add the main flower color—the rose pictured here has been colored with plum and white petal dust mixed together. Aim most of the color at the tightly spiraled center as this helps to create a focal point in the rose. Catch the outer edges of the petals gently so that the color fades more toward the outer layer of petals.

The calyx

12 Rolling out the paste
Form a ball of well-kneaded mid green gum paste into a cone shape, then pinch out the base to form a hat shape. Roll out the paste again to make it a little finer.

14 Adding details
Place the calyx on a foam pad and hollow out the length of each sepal using a ball tool. Many rose calyces have fine hairy bits to the edges of the sepals—you can add these by snipping into the edge of the calyx with fine curved scissors. The number of hairs varies between varieties, and some have no hairs at all.

13 Cutting the calyx
Cut out the calyx shape using a rose calyx cutter (see page 136 for a template). Remove the paste from the cutter and place against the nonstick board. Use a ceramic modeling tool to roll each of the sepals to thin and elongate them.

15 Placing the calyx
Open up the center of the calyx using the pointed end of the ceramic tool. Moisten the center and thread it onto the back of the rose, positioning each sepal to cover a join between petals. Curl the tips back if desired.

Leaves

16 Cutting the leaves
Leaves are made in sets of three or five depending upon the variety of rose you are making. Roll out some mid green gum paste, leaving a thick ridge for the wire—a grooved board can speed up this process greatly. Cut out the leaves using the rose leaf cutters or the template on page 136. Insert a moistened 30-, 28-, or 26-gauge wire into the leaf (depending on the size of the leaf) about halfway.

17 Veining the leaves
Soften the edges of the leaf and vein using the large rose leaf veiner. Pinch from behind the leaf to accentuate the central vein and give more movement to the leaf. Repeat to make leaves of various sizes.

18 Grouping the leaves
Tape over a little of each wire stem with quarter-width Nile green tape. Tape the leaves into sets of three or five starting with the largest leaf and two medium-sized leaves, one on either side. Finally, add the two smaller leaves at the base.

19 Coloring the leaves
Dust the edges of the leaves and the upper stems with eggplant and plum mixed together. Dust the upper surface of the leaf in layers, lightly with forest green and heavier with foliage and vine green. Dust the backs with white petal dust and the brush used for the greens. Spray the leaves lightly with edible spray varnish or dip into a half glaze.

Cut out the leaves using a rose leaf cutter (16).

Insert a moistened wire into the leaf (16).

Soften the edges of the leaf (17).

Vein and pinch to accentuate the central vein (17).

Dust the edges of the leaves with eggplant and plum petal dust (19).

Dust the upper surface with forest green, foliage, and vine green (19).

Spray with edible spray varnish or glaze (19).

Group the leaves into sets of three or five (18).

Asiatic lily

There are many types of lily suitable for wedding cakes and bridal bouquets—the flower shown here is based on one of the Asiatic varieties. The color range and potential variation in spots, stripes, and markings is huge, allowing cake decorators plenty of scope for matching their color schemes.

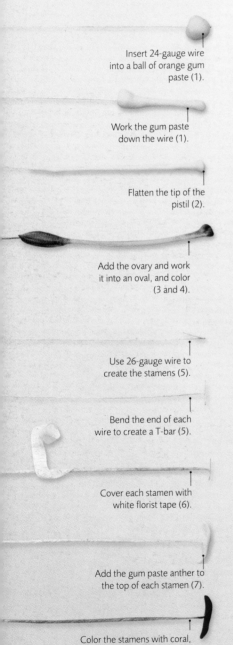

Insert 24-gauge wire into a ball of orange gum paste (1).

Work the gum paste down the wire (1).

Flatten the tip of the pistil (2).

Add the ovary and work it into an oval, and color (3 and 4).

Use 26-gauge wire to create the stamens (5).

Bend the end of each wire to create a T-bar (5).

Cover each stamen with white florist tape (6).

Add the gum paste anther to the top of each stamen (7).

Color the stamens with coral, tangerine, terra cotta, and eggplant petal dusts (8).

The pistil

1 Shaping the pistil
In this variety of lily, the pistil reflects the color of the petals. Cut a length of 24-gauge white wire in half. Insert the tip of the wire into a ball of well-kneaded orange gum paste. Hold the ball firmly between your finger and thumb and work it firmly down the wire, leaving the tip slightly rounded. You are aiming to create a length at least the same as the petal length.

2 Adding detail
Smooth the length of the pistil between your palms. Next, flatten the rounded tip of the pistil and then pinch carefully into three sections using the tweezers. Reshape each section with your fingers if the shape needs to be softened slightly. Curve the pistil gently along its length.

3 The ovary
Add a ball of mid green gum paste at the base of the pistil to represent the ovary. Work the ball into an oval shape. Divide the surface into six sections lengthways using a craft knife or the plain-edged cutting wheel.

4 Coloring the pistil
Dust the pistil with a mixture of tangerine and coral petal dust. Color the ovary with a mixture of vine and foliage green. Tinge the tip of the pistil with eggplant petal dust.

The stamens

5 Shaping the stamens
Cut two lengths of 26-gauge wire into thirds to make six lengths for the stamens. Bend each end over using needle-nose pliers and then bend this piece at the center to form a T-bar shape.

6 Taping the stamens
Tape around the length of the stamen a few times using quarter-width white florist tape. Increase the quantity of tape toward the base to create a fleshier feel.

7 Adding the anther
Form a cigar-shaped piece of orange gum paste to represent the anther. Moisten the T-bar slightly and push it into the paste. Blend and mold the paste to secure it on the wire. Divide the upper length of the anther using a craft knife. Repeat to make six stamens.

Materials

- Gum paste: orange and mid green
- 26 and 24-gauge white wires
- Petal dust: tangerine, coral, plum, foliage, vine, eggplant, and terra cotta
- White and Nile green florist tape
- Ruby liquid color

Equipment

- Small tweezers
- Craft knife or plain-edged cutting wheel
- Flat dusting brushes
- Needle-nose pliers
- Lily petal cutters (or the templates from page 137)
- Large metal ball tool
- Lily petal veiners (one wide; one narrow)
- Fine paintbrush

See page 137 for the Asiatic lily templates.

8 Coloring the stamens

Dust the length of each stamen with a mixture of coral and tangerine petal dust—try to fade the color toward the tip. Color the anther heavily with a mixture of terra cotta and eggplant petal dust. You might prefer to paint the anther with fresh egg white and then dip it into a mixture of the two dusts to create a more velvety effect—however, take care not to drop dust onto your petals or, worse still, the decorated cake surface.

9 Assembling stamens and pistil

Tape the six stamens around the pistil using half-width Nile green florist tape. Curve the length of each slightly as you position them. They should be positioned at a slightly lower level than the tip of the pistil.

The petals

10 Cutting the petals

There are three wide inner petals and three narrower outer petals. Roll out some well-kneaded orange gum paste, leaving a thick ridge for the wire (see page 101). Cut out a petal shape using a petal cutter or using a craft knife or plain-edged cutting wheel and the lily petal templates (see page 137). Insert a moistened 24-gauge wire a third to half way into the petal.

11 Finishing the petals

Soften the edges gently with a large metal ball tool. Vein the petal using a double-sided lily petal veiner. Pinch the length of the petal from the base to the tip to create a graceful curved shape. Allow it to dry over a curved surface. Repeat to make the three wide and three narrow petals. Curl the outer three narrow petals slightly more than the inner ones.

Coloring and assembly

12 Dusting the petals

Dust each petal in layers, starting with tangerine and then the coral petal dust. Add tinges of plum and eggplant to the edges. Use a fine paintbrush and ruby liquid food color to paint fine spots at the base of each petal, adding more to the inner three wide petals.

13 Finishing the bloom

Tape the three wide petals around the base of the stamens using half-width Nile green tape. Add the narrow petals next, positioning them to fill in the gaps between the inner petals.

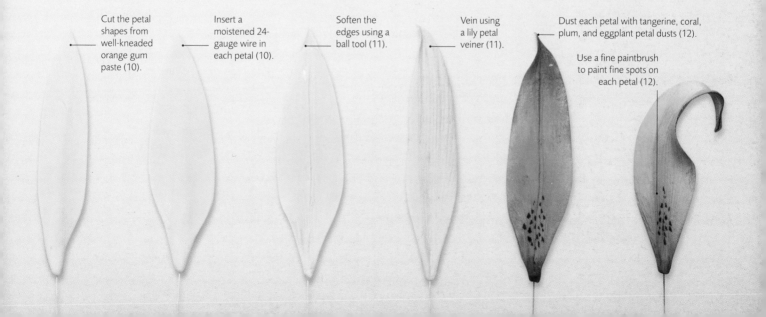

Cut the petal shapes from well-kneaded orange gum paste (10).

Insert a moistened 24-gauge wire in each petal (10).

Soften the edges using a ball tool (11).

Vein using a lily petal veiner (11).

Dust each petal with tangerine, coral, plum, and eggplant petal dusts (12).

Use a fine paintbrush to paint fine spots on each petal (12).

Calla lily

Calla lily is also known as *Zantedeschia* and is popular among florists and cake decorators. These fabulous flowers originate from Africa and have been cultivated to create many variations in color and form. They are very quick and fairly simple to make in gum paste.

The spadix

Insert 18-gauge wire into a ball of white gum paste (1).

Work the gum paste down the wire (1).

Smooth the shape between your palms (1).

Texture the spadix with a nutmeg grater (2).

Add a ball of gum paste to the base of the spadix (2).

Dip the spadix into sugartex or semolina colored with yellow petal dust (3).

1 Making the spadix
Use a full or three-quarter length of 18-gauge wire. Insert the moistened wire into a ball of well-kneaded white gum paste. Work the paste down the wire to create the required length of spadix—this will depend on the size of flower you are making and also the variety; some have very short spadix centers. Smooth the shape between your palms and then remove any excess paste from the base.

2 Texturing the surface
Texture the surface by rolling the spadix against the surface of a nutmeg grater. Add a ball of paste at the base of the spadix to help give a more padded finish to the final flower.

3 Coloring the spadix
Dust the spadix with eggplant petal dust. Paint the surface with egg white and dip into yellow sugartex or semolina colored with yellow petal dust. If you are making a white flower, or pale colored variety, color the spadix with yellow petal dust and then add yellow sugartex. Allow to dry.

Materials
- 18-gauge wire
- Gum paste: white
- Petal dust: lemon, eggplant, plum, coral, white, vine green, foliage, and white
- Egg white
- Yellow sugartex or semolina colored with yellow petal dust

Equipment
- Nutmeg grater
- Flat dusting brushes
- Calla lily cutter or template (page 137)
- Craft knife or plain-edge cutting wheel
- Foam pad
- Large metal ball tool
- Wide amaryllis petal veiner or similar
- Dresden tool

See page 137 for the calla lily templates.

The spathe

4 Forming the spathe
Roll out some white gum paste; not too thinly as this is quite a fleshy flower. Cut out the spathe shape using the calla lily cutter or template and the craft knife or plain-edge cutting wheel.

5 Softening the edges
Place the shape onto a foam pad and soften the edges using the large metal ball tool.

6 Veining
Add veins to the spathe using a wide amaryllis veiner or similar—because this is a large piece of paste you might need to vein one half of the shape and then move the paste over the veiner to texture the other half. Add extra central veins down the length of the spathe using the fine end of the Dresden tool.

7 Creating the flower
Moisten the base of the spadix with fresh egg white and then position it to one side of the spathe. Some varieties curl from the left; others from the right. Roll the spadix against the spathe to create the wrapped flower shape. Carefully curl back the edges.

8 Shaping the flower
Pinch and form a ridged vein down the back of the spathe, increasing the pressure at the tip to create a fine point.

9 Curling the edges
If the flower is very large you will need to hang it upside down to allow the paste to firm up a little more before creating the final curled-back shape. Make some flowers with a tighter wrap than others to give a more interesting overall finish to the spray.

10 Coloring
Dust the base of the spathe in layers with vine green and then foliage colors. Add a tinge of both greens at the tip. Dust the remainder of the spathe in layers of coral and plum mixed together. Add a tinge of eggplant to the edges and deep inside the throat of the flower. Allow to dry. Steam to set the color (see page 105).

Cut out the shape for the spathe (4).

Roll the spathe around the spadix (7).

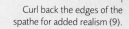

Curl back the edges of the spathe for added realism (9).

Dust the base of the spathe in green petal dust (10).

Cattleya orchid

This is a traditional American bridal orchid that works well in bouquets or on a cake. There are around 60 species of Cattleya orchids that originate from the rain forests of South America. There are many more cultivated hybrids that produce beautiful showy flowers and are often used in bridal bouquets. The color range is vast, from pure white (shown here) through to hybrids with very vibrant throats and clashing colored outer petals.

Column

Roll a ball of well-kneaded gum paste (1).

Insert a wire into the teardrop shape (1).

Hollow out the underside of the column (2).

Pinch a ridge down the back and curve the shape slightly (2).

Add a tiny ball of paste to the top of the anther (3).

1 Forming the column
This is the central part of the flower that holds the throat petal. It is best to make this in advance and allow it to dry before adding the weight of the lip. Roll a ball of well-kneaded white gum paste. Form the ball into a teardrop shape and insert a moistened 22-gauge wire into the pointed end to support most of the length of the shape.

2 Shaping the column
Hollow out the underside of the column by placing it against the rounded smooth end of the silk veining tool. Firmly press the shape against the tool, pinching a gentle ridge down the back with your finger and thumb as you work. Curve the length of the shape slightly.

3 Making the anther cap
Add a tiny ball of paste to represent the anther cap at the tip of the column. Divide the cap into two sections using a craft knife. Set aside to dry.

Materials
- Gum paste: white
- 26-, 24-, and 22- gauge white wires
- Petal dust: lemon, primrose, white, vine-green, and foliage
- Nile green florist tape

Equipment
- Ceramic silk veining tool
- Craft knife
- Cattleya orchid cutters or templates (see page 137)
- Amaryllis petal veiner or similar fan-shaped petal veiner
- Nonstick board
- Dresden tool
- Paper towel
- Soft-veined petal veiner
- Dusting brushes

See page 137 for the Cattleya orchid templates.

Throat petal

4 Cutting the throat petal
Roll out some gum paste, leaving a thick ridge (see page 101). The paste needs to be quite fleshy for this part of the flower, to help you create a heavily frilled throat. Cut out the throat shape using the template and a craft knife or a Cattleya orchid throat cutter.

5 Veining the throat petal
Place the throat petal into a double-sided amaryllis veiner and press firmly to create a heavily veined effect. Remove the petal from the veiner and place onto the nonstick board.

Cut out and vein the throat petal (4 and 5).

6 Frilling the edge
Use the broad end of the Dresden tool to pull out the edge of the paste at intervals to create a heavy double-frilled effect. Next, soften the frill using the silk veining tool—again, working at intervals over the frill, but this time using a rolling action.

7 Assembling the throat and column
Moisten the base of the throat petal and carefully wrap it around the dried column, making sure the column is positioned with the hollowed side down against the petal. Overlap the petal at the base and then curl back the edges slightly. There should be some space between the underside of the column and the petal—this can be added by opening up the area using the broad end of the Dresden tool. Leave to dry before coloring. The throat might need supporting with a ring of paper towel while it dries (see page 102).

Pull out the petal edge to create a double-frilled effect (6).

The wing petals

8 Cutting out the sepals
Roll out some gum paste, leaving a thick ridge down the center. Cut out the petal using the wing template from page 137, and a craft knife, or a Cattleya wing cutter.

9 Wiring the wing petals
Insert a moistened 24-gauge white wire into the thick ridge so that it holds about a third to half the length of each wing petal.

10 Veining the petals
Vein the petals using the amaryllis veiner. Frill the edges using the silk veining tool. Pinch a subtle ridge down the center of each petal. Allow them to dry over a gentle curve of paper towel.

Wrap the throat petal around the column (7).

Cut out the petals using a Cattleya wing cutter or scalpel (8).

Frill the edges of the wing petals as you did for the throat petal (10).

Curl back the edges of the throat petal (7).

Outer sepals

Soften the edges of the sepals with a ball tool (12).

11 Cutting out the sepals

You will need to make three outer sepals. Roll out the gum paste leaving a thick ridge as before. Cut out the sepal shape using a craft knife and the templates from page 137 or a Cattleya sepal cutter.

12 Wiring and veining

Insert a moistened 26-gauge white wire into the thick ridge. Soften the edges using a large ball tool. Vein using a soft-veined petal veiner. Repeat to make the three sepals. Dry one sepal forward to represent the dorsal sepal and the other two curved back for the lateral sepals.

Dry two of the sepals curved backward (12).

Coloring and assembly

13 Coloring the throat

Add a mixture of lemon and primrose petal dust deep in the base of the throat petal.

14 Assembling the flower

Tape the two wing petals onto either side of the throat petal using half-width Nile green florist tape. Next add the dorsal sepal to curve behind the wing petals and finally the lateral sepals at the base of the flower.

15 Finishing touches

Mix together vine, white, and a little foliage green petal dust and add tinges to the base and tip of each sepal.

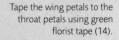

Tape the wing petals to the throat petals using green florist tape (14).

Fern

Ferns are wonderful space fillers in a bridal bouquet. They are fairly simple to make although they do tend to be very fragile when dry, so it is best to make them just before you need to add them to an arrangement or bouquet.

Fern frond

1 Cutting the fern leaf
Roll out a large ball of well-kneaded mid green gum paste, not too thinly. Cut out the fern leaf using the ladder fern cutter or the template on page 138. As this is a tricky shape it is often best to place the paste on top of the cutter and roll over the top of it with a nonstick rolling pin.

2 Frilling and veining
Remove the paste from the cutter and place it against the nonstick board. Using the broad end of the Dresden veining tool, work both edges of each frond—press and drag the paste from the frond edges against the board to create a double-frilled, veined effect.

3 Adding the central veins
Place the fern on a firm foam pad and, using the fine end of the Dresden veining tool, create a central vein down the length of each section.

4 Wiring the fern
Tape over the length of a 24-gauge wire with quarter-width Nile green florist tape. Paint the wire to the length of the leaf with fresh egg white. Place the moistened wire on top of the fern leaf so that it runs down the center of the shape. Press it firmly to secure.

5 Shaping the fern
Quickly flip the fern over and use angled tweezers to pinch the paste onto either side of the wire to secure it in place. Flip the frond back over and bend it to create an attractive shape. Pinch the tips of each section to create movement.

6 Coloring
It is best to dust the fern before it has a chance to dry using layers of foliage green and then vine green petal dust. Older ferns can be darker in color if desired. Ferns also look good sprayed gold or silver for Christmas wedding designs.

Materials
- Gum paste: mid green
- 24-gauge white wire
- Nile green florist tape
- Egg white
- Petal dust: vine green and foliage

Equipment
- Ladder fern cutter
- Nonstick rolling pin
- Nonstick board
- Foam pad
- Dresden tool
- Flat dusting brush
- Angled tweezers

See page 138 for the fern templates.

Cut out the fern using a cutter and frill each of the fronds (1 and 2).

Attached a wire to the fern and pinch the paste either side of the wire (4 and 5).

Ruscus

Ruscus provides foliage that is very quick and easy to make, using a freestyle technique without cutters. There are several varieties of Ruscus—the one shown here is one of the smaller forms.

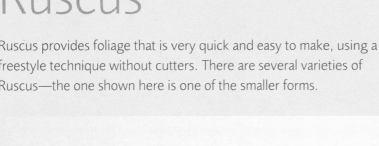

Insert a wire into a teardrop-shaped piece of gum paste (2).

Work the paste onto the wire (2).

Flatten the teardrop against a nonstick board (3).

Texture the leaf with a veiner (4).

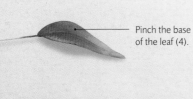
Pinch the base of the leaf (4).

Dust each leaf with forest green, foliage, and vine green (5).

Glaze with edible spray or half-glaze (5).

1 Cutting wire lengths
Cut lengths of 33-, 30-, or 28-gauge white wire into thirds (the thickness will depend on the size of leaf you plan to make).

2 Putting the paste on the wire
Roll a ball of mid green gum paste and form it into a slender teardrop shape. Insert a wire into the broad end of the teardrop. Work the paste onto the wire and then place against the nonstick board.

3 Flattening the leaf
Flatten the teardrop against the board using the flat side of the veiner. This should leave you with a larger, thinner leaf shape. You might need to trim the edges with sharp scissors to create the exact shape you desire (see page 138 for a template).

4 Shaping the leaf
Place the leaf into the veiner to texture the surface. Remove the leaf from the veiner and pinch it at the base and the tip to accentuate a central vein and give the leaf some movement. Repeat to make as many leaves as desired.

5 Finishing the leaves
Dust each leaf lightly with forest green, and then overdust heavily using foliage and vine green. Glaze using half-glaze or edible spray varnish. Tape the leaves into sets of three, using half-width Nile green florist tape.

Materials
- 33-, 30-, and 28-gauge white wires
- Gum paste: mid green
- Petal dust: forest, foliage, and vine green
- Half-glaze or edible spray varnish
- Nile green florist tape

Equipment
- Nonstick board
- Petal veiner
- Sharp scissors
- Flat dusting brushes

See page 138 for the Ruscus templates.

Ivy

Used to symbolize fertility, ivy seems to be the most popular foliage for both bridal bouquets and wedding cakes. Trailing stems are fairly quick to create and fill space attractively on cakes.

The leaves

1 Cutting the leaves
Roll out some mid green gum paste on a grooved board. The thickness will depend on the size of the leaf you are making. Cut out the desired leaf size using one of the ivy cutters—they are usually in sets of three or four. Alternatively, see page 138 for ivy leaf templates.

2 Inserting the stems
Insert a moistened wire into the thick ridge of the leaf. The gauge of the wire will depend upon the size of the leaf: 33-gauge wire for tiny leaves; 30-gauge for medium leaves; and 28-gauge for larger leaves.

3 Softening the edges
Soften the edges of the leaf with a medium metal ball tool and then vein them with the double-sided ivy (or nasturtium) leaf veiner.

4 Finishing the leaves
Pinch the leaf from the base to the tip and each of its points to give it a more three-dimensional, realistic effect. Repeat to make numerous leaves.

Coloring and assembly

5 Coloring the leaves
Use the brush to tinge the edge of each leaf with eggplant petal dust. Next, dust each leaf in layers—start very lightly with forest green, then dust heavily with foliage green. Allow the leaves to dry.

6 Glazing the leaves
Dip each leaf into a half-glaze or spray lightly with an edible spray varnish (see page 105). Tape over each leaf stem with quarter-width Nile green florist tape.

7 Finishing the arrangement
Tape over the end of a 24-gauge wire with half-width Nile green florist tape. Curl the end around a paintbrush to create a tendril effect that represents new growth. Add a small leaf to the stem, leaving part of its stem on show. Add more leaves down the trailing stem, gradating the leaf size as you work. You might need to introduce additional 24-gauge wires to create extra support for longer ivy trails. Bend the whole length of the stem to create movement. Dust the main stem lightly with eggplant and foliage dusts.

Materials
- Gum paste: mid green
- 33-, 30-, 28-, and 24-gauge white wires
- Nile green florist tape
- Petal dust: foliage, forest, and eggplant
- Half-glaze or edible spray varnish (see page 105)

Equipment
- Grooved board
- Ivy leaf cutters
- Medium metal ball tool
- Ivy leaf or nasturtium leaf veiners
- Flat dusting brush

See page 138 for the ivy template.

Cut out the leaf shape using an ivy cutter (1).

Insert a moistened wire into the leaf (2).

Soften and vein the leaf (3).

Pinch the leaf from base to tip (4).

Dust each leaf with forest and foliage green (5).

Glaze with half-glaze or edible spray varnish (6).

Tape the stem with Nile green florist tape (7).

Recipes

Here, you'll find handy recipes for buttercream, royal icing, and gum paste, as well as recipes for a high-density sponge cake and fruitcake.

Buttercream

You can vary the proportion of butter to sugar according to taste—for a very creamy buttercream (sometimes called French buttercream), use equal amounts of butter and sugar. This recipe uses a larger proportion of sugar for a more resilient icing.

Ingredients

- ¹/₂ cup (125 g) shortening
- ¹/₂ cup (125 g) unsalted butter, softened
- 1 teaspoon vanilla extract
- 4 cups (1 kg) confectioner's sugar
- 2 tablespoons milk

Basic recipe

In a large bowl, cream together the butter, shortening, and vanilla. Blend in the sugar, one cup at a time, beating well after each addition. Beat in the milk, and continue mixing until light and fluffy. Keep icing covered until ready to decorate.

FLAVORINGS

Citrus: try adding about 5 tablespoons of lemon or orange curd to the basic buttercream recipe—the exact amount will depend on your taste. Alternately, replace the milk and vanilla extract with orange or lemon juice and a couple of teaspoons of grated lemon or orange rind.

Floral twist: try adding lavender or rose syrup flavorings to the basic recipe—again, omit the vanilla and the milk.

White or plain chocolate: replace half the amount of butter in the basic recipe with chocolate that has been melted in a bowl over hot water and left to cool slightly. Add the melted chocolate to the buttercream and beat them together.

Irish cream: add a cream liqueur according to taste; but try not to alter the consistency of the buttercream too much.

Coffee: blend two teaspoons of good quality instant coffee with one teaspoon of boiling water, or use strong expresso coffee, and add it to the buttercream.

Milk chocolate: use melted chocolate, as for white or plain chocolate buttercream, or blend two tablespoons of unsweetened cocoa powder with two tablespoons of boiling water. Leave the mixture to cool before adding to the buttercream.

Royal icing

Royal icing is strong enough for lace, filigree, and extension work. The addition of tartaric and acetic acids alters the pH balance of the egg white to help give it strength. Omitting the acids gives an icing that is suitable for piping fine embroidery and brush embroidery.

Ingredients

- 1 medium egg white, free range and at room temperature
- Pinch of tartaric acid (for fine lace work) or two drops of acetic acid (for long, dropped lines of extension work)
- 1¹/₂ cups (225 g) confectioner's sugar, sifted

Royal icing with fresh egg white

1 Wash your mixing bowl and beater with a concentrated detergent and then scald them to remove any traces of grease and leftover detergent.

2 Place the egg white into the mixer bowl with most of the confectioner's sugar, and mix the two together.

3 Fix the bowl and beater to the machine and beat on the slowest speed until the icing has reached full peak consistency (the icing should stand up in peaks)—this will take around eight minutes. You might need to add a little extra sugar if the mixture is too soft.

Ingredients

- 3 tablespoons pure dried albumen powder
- 1¹/₄ cups (315 ml) water
- 10¹/₂ cups (1.75 kg) confectioner's sugar

Royal icing with dried albumen

This royal icing recipe is suitable for coating, piping, run-outs, and brush embroidery. There are several types of dried albumen powders available, so check the instructions on the packet for proportions and mixing times.

1 Wash the mixing bowl, a second smaller bowl, and the beater from the machine with a concentrated detergent and scald to remove any grease or leftover detergent.

2 Reconstitute the dried albumen with the water in a small bowl. It will become very lumpy, but don't worry, just stir and leave it to dissolve for 20 minutes (or longer if you have time). Strain the mixture into the mixer bowl.

3 Add the sifted confectioner's sugar gradually and mix it into the albumen. Fix the bowl and beater to the electric mixer and beat on the slowest speed until the icing reaches soft peak consistency, which is ideal for coating a cake. Alternatively, continue to mix until the icing is much stiffer—what is known as full peak consistency. Store the icing in an airtight container. This icing can be beaten the following day to bring it back to the correct consistency.

Gum paste

Gum paste is ideal for creating handmade flowers and other three-dimensional decorations. It is convenient to buy ready-made commercial gum paste and this tends to be more consistent than mixing your own. The type of paste you choose will depends on your personal preference. For example, paste that stretches well and does not dry out too quickly will allow you to work on a flower for longer, though many people prefer a firmer paste... each to their own! The following is a good, basic gum paste recipe for times when you do need to mix your own. Gum tragacanth gives the paste stretch and strength. This paste can also be mixed with fondant to create a paste suitable for modeling fine frills, swags, and drapes.

Ingredients

- 5 teaspoons cold water
- 2 teaspoons powdered gelatine
- 3 cups (500 g) confectioner's sugar, sifted
- 3 teaspoons gum tragacanth
- 2 teaspoons liquid glucose
- 3 teaspoons white vegetable shortening, plus an extra teaspoon to add later
- 1 large fresh egg white

1 Mixing

Mix the cold water and gelatine together in a small bowl and leave to stand for 30 minutes. Sift the icing sugar and gum tragacanth together into the bowl of a heavy-duty mixer and fit it into the machine.

2 Heating

Place the bowl containing the gelatine mixture over a saucepan of hot water and stir until the gelatine has dissolved. Warm a teaspoon in hot water and then measure out the liquid glucose—the heat from the spoon should help the glucose to dissolve more quickly. Add the glucose and shortening to the gelatine mixture and continue to heat until all the ingredients have dissolved.

3 Beating

Add the dissolved mixture to the icing sugar with the egg white. Fit the beater to the machine and turn it to its lowest speed. Gradually increase the speed to maximum to until the paste is white and stringy.

4 Kneading and storing

Remove the paste from the bowl, knead together, and cover using the remaining teaspoon of shortening—this helps to keep the paste from forming a dry crust that can leave hard bits in the paste at the rolling-out stage. Place the paste in a plastic bag and store it in an airtight container. Allow the paste to rest for twelve hours before using it.

High-density sponge cake

High-density sponge cake is ideal for wedding cakes as it is light and delicious to eat but firm enough to be carved or stacked for decorating, but remember to use dowels for support if you do want to stack a sponge cake. This recipe makes a 10-in. (25-cm) round cake.

Ingredients

- 4 cups (500 g) cake flour
- 4 teaspoons baking powder
- 2¹/₂ cups (570 g) superfine sugar
- 2 cups (500 g) shortening or butter (soft to the touch)
- ¹/₃ cup (75 ml) cold water
- 3 cups (500 g) eggs (around nine—crack and weigh them without shells)

1 Preheat the oven. Fan-assisted oven: 285°F, gas mark 2 (145°C).
Regular oven: 350°F, gas mark 4 (180°C).

2 Place all the cake ingredients in a mixing bowl. Mix on a slow speed until there are no lumps of fat visible.

3 Scrape any mixture that has risen up the sides of the bowl back down, and mix on a medium speed for two minutes.

4 Scrape the mixture down into the bottom of the bowl again, then mix on full speed for a further minute.

5 Spoon the mixture into a 10-in. (25-cm) round pan, and bake for around one hour 20 minutes or until it is cooked.

6 Leave the cake to cool on a cooling rack.

TIPS

- Your butter or shortening and eggs should be at room temperature. Leave them out of the fridge for about 6 hours prior to making the cake.
- Wrap the cake pan in wet newspaper or baking strips to keep the cake from over-cooking or catching on the sides.

HIGH-DENSITY SPONGE VARIATIONS

- For a lemon or orange sponge: add the zest from four unwaxed lemons or oranges and replace the water in the recipe with the same amount of lemon or orange juice.
- Sprinkle the cooked cake with a lemon or orange syrup:
  2 tablespoons superfine sugar
  2 tablespoons hot water
  2 tablespoons lemon or orange juice
- Irish cream cake—add a double amount of Irish cream liqueur to replace the water in the recipe. Sprinkle the cooked cake with Irish cream liqueur prior to filling and decorating it.
- Mocha cake—replace 5 oz (140 g) of the flour with good quality cocoa powder. Add ¹/₂ teaspoon baking powder and replace the water with diluted coffee.

Fruitcake

Fruitcake is a favored base in the UK, you may be asked to make one. This fruitcake recipe will fill a 12 in. (30 cm) square cake pan exactly or a 12 in. (30 cm) round cake pan with some left over for another, smaller cake. Double the recipe for a three-tier cake and line an extra smaller tin in case there is more mixture than you require. The variety and amount of each type of dried fruit can be changed to suit your taste—if you are not a fan of prunes or figs, replace them with another fruit.

Ingredients

- 8 cups (1 kg) raisins
- 8 cups (1 kg) sultanas
- 4 cups (500 g) dried figs, chopped
- 4 cups (500 g) dried prunes, chopped
- 2 cups (250 g) natural color glacé cherries, halved
- 1 cup (125 g) dried apricots, chopped
- 1 cup (125 g) dried or glacé pineapple, chopped
- Zest and juice of one orange
- ³/₄ cup (200 ml) brandy (or Cointreau or cherry brandy)
- 2 cups (500 g) unsalted butter, at room temperature
- 2 cups (250 g) light muscovado sugar
- 2 cups (250 g) dark muscovado sugar
- 4 teaspoons of apricot jam
- 8 teaspoons of golden syrup
- 1 teaspoon each of ground ginger, allspice, nutmeg, cloves, and cinnamon
- ¹/₂ teaspoon of ground mace
- 4 cups (500 g) plain flour
- 2 cups (250 g) ground almonds
- 10 large free range eggs, at room temperature

1 Use a large pair of scissors to halve and chop the dried fruit. Mix the dried fruit, orange zest, orange juice, and alcohol together in a plastic container with a lid. Seal the container and leave to soak for about a week, if time allows, or for as long as you have.

2 Cream the butter in a large bowl until soft. Gradually add the sugars and beat the two together. Stir in the apricot jam, golden syrup, and spices.

3 Sift the flour into a separate bowl and stir in the almonds.

4 Beat the eggs and add them slowly to the butter and sugar mixture, alternating it with the flour and almond mixture. Don't add the eggs too quickly because they might curdle.

5 Before you add the fruit, set aside a small amount of batter—this is to use on top of the fruited batter to stop the fruit from burning in the oven. Mix the soaked fruit into the larger amount of batter. Grease and line the pan(s) with baking parchment. Fill the pan with batter to the required depth—usually about two-thirds of the depth. Apply a thin layer of the unfruited batter on top and smooth over. Bake at 275°F (140°C) for four to six hours, depending on the size of the cake. The cake will shrink slightly away from the sides of the pan, and will feel firm to the touch and smell wonderful. If in doubt, test with a skewer—if it comes out clean, the cake is ready.

6 Allow the cake to cool slightly in the pan, add a couple of extra dashes of alcohol, and then leave it to cool completely. Store the cake wrapped in baking parchment and clingwrap. Leave it to mature for as long as you can—a few days up to a few months works well.

Templates

The templates illustrated here will help you to complete the various projects contained in the book. The designs can be reduced or increased in size using a photocopier. Trace the designs onto tracing paper and scribe gently into the icing—through the paper—using a scriber, pin, or a ballpoint pen that has run out of ink. Templates for flowers and leaves are best cut out from thin plastic, you could buy some from a crafts store or use empty margarine or ice cream containers.

Silver hearts, page 57

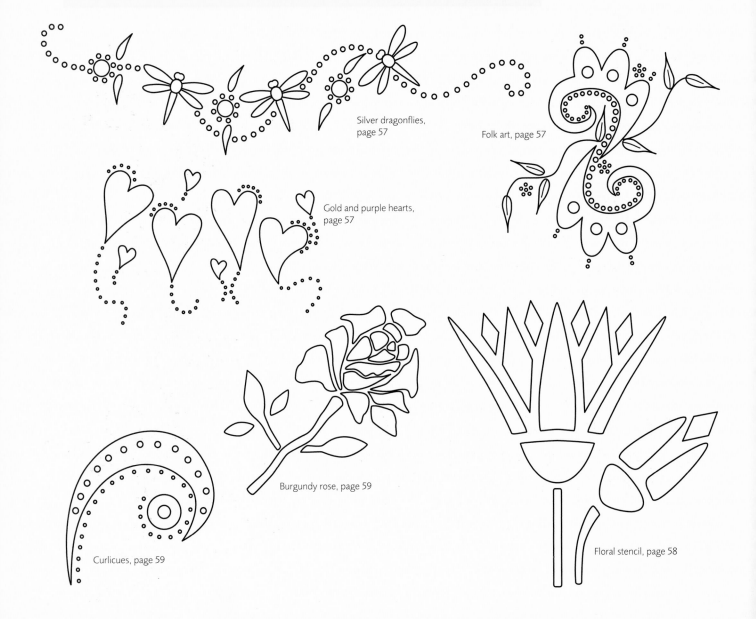

Silver dragonflies, page 57

Folk art, page 57

Gold and purple hearts, page 57

Burgundy rose, page 59

Curlicues, page 59

Floral stencil, page 58

Dusky rose, page 67

Sequin and rose, page 67

Fine dots, page 67

Wild rose, page 69

Golden rose, page 67

Almond blossom, page 69

Viola, page 69

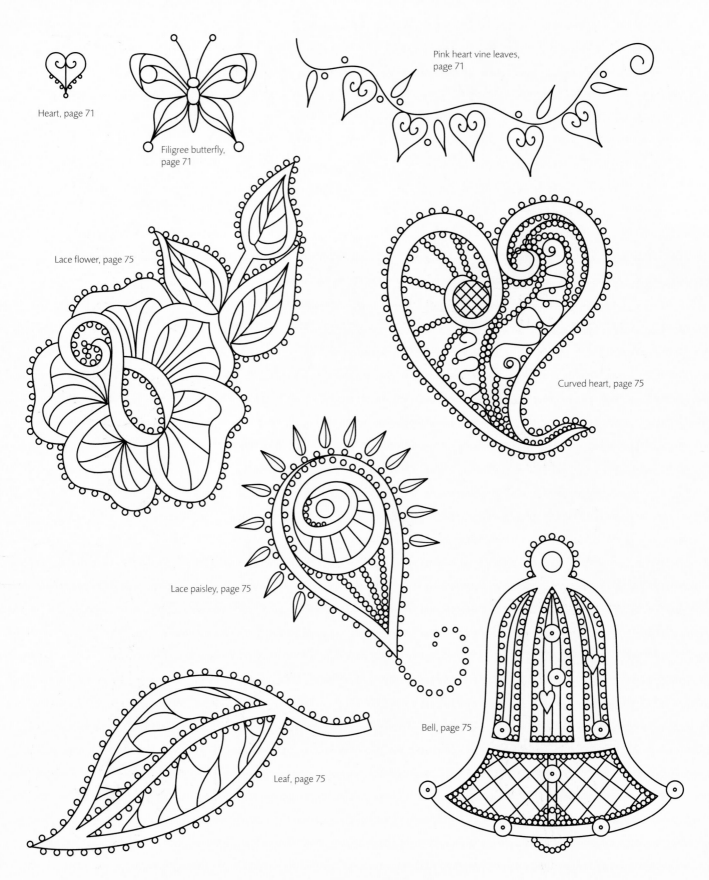

Heart, page 71

Filigree butterfly,
page 71

Pink heart vine leaves,
page 71

Lace flower, page 75

Curved heart, page 75

Lace paisley, page 75

Leaf, page 75

Bell, page 75

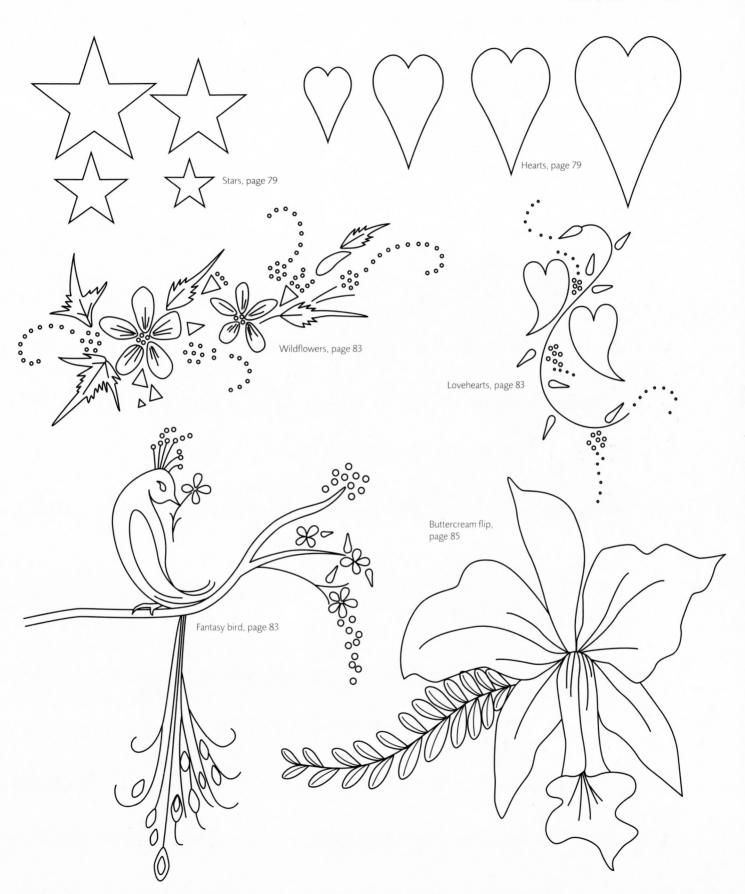

Stars, page 79

Hearts, page 79

Wildflowers, page 83

Lovehearts, page 83

Buttercream flip, page 85

Fantasy bird, page 83

Trailing blossom,
page 108

Open rose petals,
page 110

Formal rose petals,
page 112

Rose leaves, page 115

Rose calyces, page 114

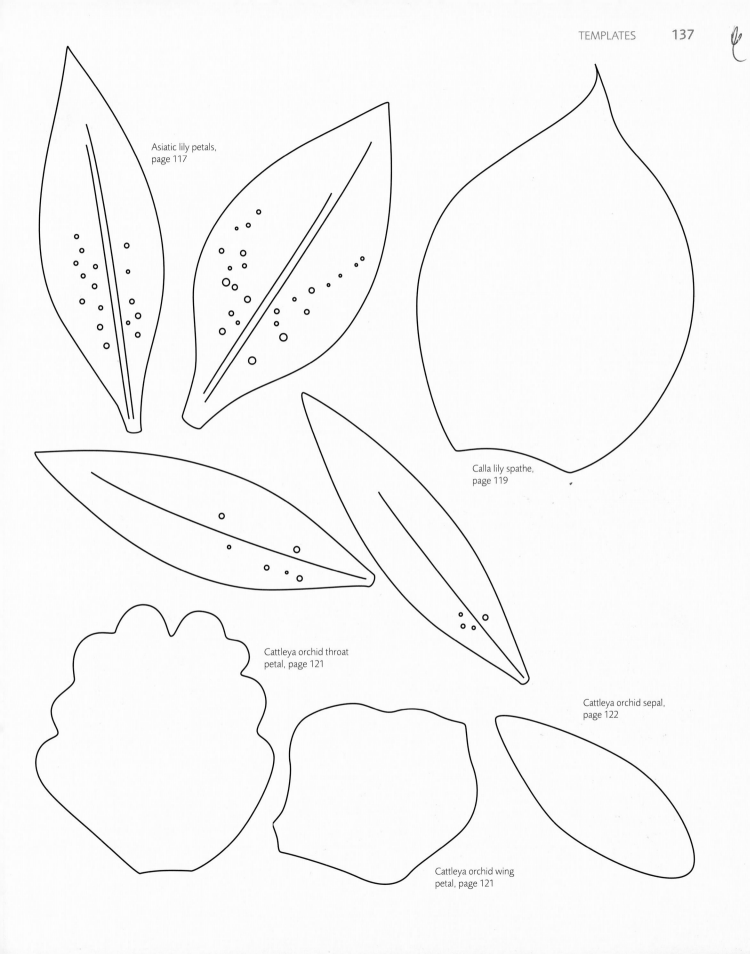

Asiatic lily petals,
page 117

Calla lily spathe,
page 119

Cattleya orchid throat
petal, page 121

Cattleya orchid sepal,
page 122

Cattleya orchid wing
petal, page 121

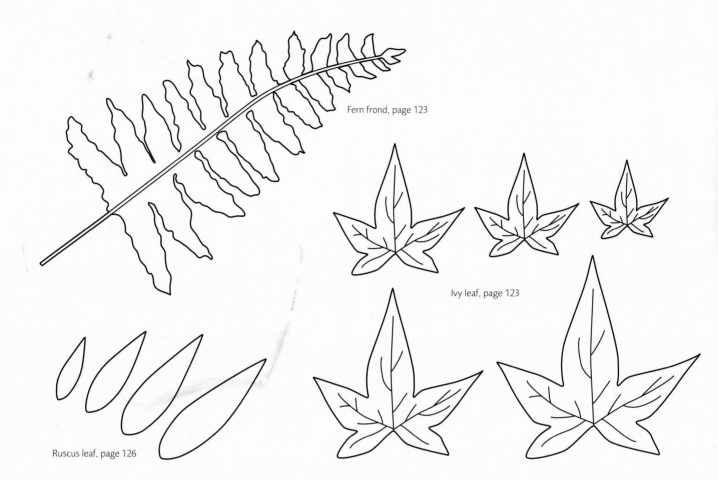

Fern frond, page 123

Ivy leaf, page 123

Ruscus leaf, page 126

Contacts

International Cake Exploration Societé
(ICES) Annual Show
ICES
4883 Camellia Lane
Bossier City, LA
71111-5424 USA
www.ices.org

**American Cake
Decorating Magazine**
4215 White Bear Parkway
Suite 100
St Paul, MN
55110-7635 USA
Tel: 651-293-1544
www.americancakedecorating.com

**Cake Decorators
School and Supplies**
244 Hall Avenue
Meriden, CT 06451
Tel: 203-634-1716
www.cakedecorators.com

Cake Carousel
1002 N. Central Expressway
Suite 501
Richardson, TX 75080
Tel: 972-690-4628
or 877-814-6670
www.cakecarousel.com

Confectionately Yours
2855 Johnson Drive, Unit X
Ventura, CA 93003
Tel: 805-650-9592
www.econfectionatelyyours.com

Wilton
Wilton Industries, Inc
2240 West 75th Street
Woodridge
IL 60517
Tel: 630-963-7100
www.wilton.com

**Michaels, The Arts
and Crafts Store**
Michaels Stores Inc.
8000 Bent Branch Dr.
Irving, TX 75063
Tel: 1-800-642-4235
www.michaels.com

Sugarcraft, Inc.
2715 Dixie Hwy.
Hamilton, OH 45015
Tel: 513-896-7089
www.sugarcraft.com

Alan Dunn
www.alandunnsugarcraft.com

Earlene Moore
www.earlenescakes.com

Cutting the cake

It can be a daunting task trying to figure out the size of cake and the tiers required to feed the number of wedding guests. The information detailed here is an approximate guide to use during the early stages of planning a wedding cake design. Note that some cake shapes are not available in certain sizes.

SIZE OF CAKE	NUMBER OF SLICES			
	ROUND		SQUARE	
SINGLE TIER	FRUIT	SPONGE	FRUIT	SPONGE
5 in. (13 cm)	14	7	16	8
6 in. (15 cm)	22	11	28	14
7 in. (18 cm)	30	15	40	20
8 in. (20 cm)	40	20	54	27
9 in. (23 cm)	54	27	70	35
10 in. (25 cm)	68	34	90	45
11 in. (27.5 cm)	86	43	112	56
12 in. (30 cm)	100	50	134	67
TWO TIER				
6 in. (15 cm) + 9 in. (23 cm)	76	38	82	41
8 in. (20 cm) + 10 in. (25 cm)	108	54	144	72
9 in. (23 cm) + 12 in. (30 cm)	154	77	204	102
THREE TIER				
6 in. (15 cm) + 8 in. (20 cm) + 10 in. (25 cm)	130	65	170	85
6 in. (15 cm) + 9 in. (23 cm) + 12 in. (30 cm)	176	88	232	116
8 in. (20 cm) + 10 in. (25 cm) + 12 in. (30 cm)	208	104	278	139
FOUR TIER				
6 in. (15 cm) + 8 in. (20 cm) + 10 in. (25 cm) + 12 in. (30 cm)	230	115	304	152

SIZE OF CAKE	NUMBER OF SLICES			
	PETAL, HEART, OCTAGON		TEARDROP	
	FRUIT	SPONGE	FRUIT	SPONGE
SINGLE TIER				
6 in. (15 cm)	15	8	10	5
7 in. (18 cm)	24	12		
8 in. (20 cm)	35	17	25	12
9 in. (23 cm)	47	24		
10 in. (25 cm)	60	30	45	22
11 in. (27.5 cm)	75	38	95	48
TWO TIER				
6 in. (15 cm) + 9 in. (23 cm)	62	32		
8 in. (20 cm) + 10 in. (25 cm)	95	47	70	34
9 in. (23 cm) + 12 in. (30 cm)	142	72		
THREE TIER				
6 in. (15 cm) + 8 in. (20 cm) + 10 in. (25 cm)	110	55	80	39
6 in. (15 cm) + 9 in. (23 cm) + 12 in. (30 cm)	157	80		
8 in. (20 cm) + 10 in. (25 cm) + 12 in. (30 cm)	190	95	145	66
FOUR TIER				
6 in. (15 cm) + 8 in. (20 cm) + 10 in. (25 cm) + 12 in. (30 cm)	205	103	155	71

SIZE OF CAKE	NUMBER OF SLICES			
	OVAL		OBLONG	
	FRUIT	SPONGE	FRUIT	SPONGE
SINGLE TIER				
4 in. (10 cm) x 6 in. (15 cm)	14	7	20	10
6 in. (15 cm) x 8 in. (20 cm)	34	17	45	22
8 in. (20 cm) x 10 in. (25 cm)	60	30	77	38
10 in. (25 cm) x 12 in. (30 cm)	96	48	115	57
TWO TIER				
6 in. (15 cm) x 8 in. (20 cm) + 8 in. (20 cm) x 10 in. (25 cm)	94		122	60
8 in. (20 cm) x 10 in. (25 cm) + 10 in. (25 cm) x 12 in. (30 cm)	156		192	95
THREE TIER				
6 in. (15 cm) x 8 in. (20 cm) + 8 in. (20 cm) x 10 in. (25 cm) + 10 in. (25 cm) x 12 in. (30 cm)	190	95	237	117
FOUR TIER				
4 in. (10 cm) x 6 in. (15 cm) + 6 in. (15 cm) x 8 in. (20 cm) + 8 in. (20 cm) x 10 in. (25 cm) + 10 in. (25 cm) x 12 in. (30 cm)	204	102	247	122

Index

Acknowledgments

Dedicated to Myrtle at number eight.

This book has been an interesting adventure and would not have been possible without help from the following people.

Thank you to Alex Julian, Ann Parker, and Jan Berry for allowing me to use their beautiful three-tier royal-iced wedding cake (page 4). Thanks to Elaine MacGregor for allowing the inclusion of the coating with royal icing sequence (pages 25–27), and to Willie Pike for his chocolate triangle cake (page 86). High-density sponge cake recipe and cake cutting advice was kindly supplied by The Dinosaur, Carole Lowe and many other sugar enthusiasts from www.bsguk.org—an amazing forum. As always none of this would be possible without the never-ending supply of help, support, and advice from Kristofer Kerrigan-Graham, Alice Christie, Tombi Peck, Sathya, Sheila Lampkin, LeeAnn Hagel, Chiyo, and last but not least, my folks!

Thank you also to the guys who worked so hard creating this book—Lindsay Kaubi and Kate Kirby in editorial, Phil Wilkins for the thousand and one photographs, and the design team, Julie Francis and Anna Plucinska, for making sense of them all.

An enormous thank you to Renshaw for supplying the Regal Ice used to create the decorations in this book.

www.renshawscott.co.uk

Many thanks also to the following suppliers, who kindly contributed toward the equipment and materials.

www.celcrafts.co.uk
www.apieceofcakethame.co.uk
www.squires-shop.com
www.patchworkcutters.com
www.design-a-cake.co.uk
www.pmeltd.co.uk
www.celebrations-teamvalley.co.uk
allan.erhorn@tiscali.co.uk
enquiries@hollyproducts.co.uk